Air

Riding the ^ Waves

Five Decades in the Public Eye. . .

and Counting

by
Eleanor Schano

About This Book

It is of vital importance that I share with you, my dear and respected readers, the methods and standards I used to write this book.

The dates, the times, the events, the people mentioned are accurate in every detail to the best of my memory.

Since archival material about the earliest days of television is scarce I had to rely on my personal recollections which could have somewhat been dimmed by the passage of time.

If I have, in any way, overlooked anybody or mis-stated any fact, I apologize.

I have been vigilant about preserving my own history, someone can always come along and try to correct my memory but the fact remains, this is my story and I told it as honestly and candidly as possible.

To Eleanor
&
Love,
Mother

This book is dedicated to my Mother
The original Eleanor Martha Schano
Who possessed the power to protect us
The vision to guide us
And the love to surround us.

●

First Edition

Pittsburgh * PA

Riding the *Air* ^ Waves:
Five Decades in the Public Eye. . . and Counting
By Eleanor Schano

Table of Contents

Breathing Life Into a Dream

Acknowledgments

Since its inception, this book has undergone many permutations and the project never could have been brought to life without the generous help of many wonderful people, to whom I offer my gratitude now.

My endless appreciation goes to Gina Catanzarite, editor in chief, who guided me gently but firmly through the process of rewriting and editing. Her enthusiasm, professional talents, and constructive criticism were critical in bringing this book to its final form.

I forever will be indebted to Patty Kreamer, who never lost faith in me. Her steady moral support and wise suggestions sustained me from the beginning to the end of this adventure. Her sincere interest and tireless efforts were demonstrated by hundreds of phone calls and emails.

My gratitude also goes to the prolific author Jim O'Brien, who was always there to offer words of encouragement.

Many thanks to Gerry Hamilton production editor/copy editor, who demonstrated great critical observations in the final edit. Special thanks to Denise Maiden and Cathy Pawlowski of Cold-Comp and Keith Maiden of Geyer Printing.

Since it has taken a lifetime to synthesize the contents of this book, I gratefully thank all of the people who have contributed to enriching my life. If writing this book was hard, then finishing it felt nearly impossible. Just when I was ready to type "The End" I'd think of one more anecdote, one more person who touched my heart, inspired my career, appeared like an angel and changed the course of my life. People have crossed my path for short periods and long, often touching my life in meaningful ways, so to anyone I have failed to recognize in my writing, I truly apologize. Know that you always are in my heart, even if you are not in the pages of this book.

Finally, I thank the people I love most in this world: My family.

To my children, especially my daughters Jennifer and Lorie, who encouraged me to take on the challenge of writing about some very personal and painful parts of our lives, I say thank you. In telling my story I also told part of your own personal history. Know that the final responsibility for what is in this book is mine.

I also want to note that no matter what accomplishments I have achieved, there have been people helping me, and for most of the past quarter-century, that person has been my husband Jack. He has been my rock, my strength, my courage through the darkest times.

In our family, Jack Feeney is the moral compass by which we all live our lives. His principled ideals, his keen wisdom, his intellectual balance has provided the sounding board I needed to move forward with my personal goals. Jack has never wavered in his loyalty and support as I went through the difficult process of writing my life story, and as I express my gratitude, I become even more deeply aware that I could not have completed this project without his sanity, patience, and advice to keep me going whenever I felt like giving up.

So, from the bottom of my heart, I thank my children, my grandchildren, and most of all, my partner, my soul mate, and my best friend . . . my husband Jack.

Prologue

*O*nce, after I had been working in the Pittsburgh television market for several decades, a viewer stopped former KDKA radio personality Wendy King in a supermarket. This isn't uncommon for members of the media. Viewers come up to us all the time to chat.

"Do you know Eleanor Schano?" the viewer asked.

Wendy, who was a personal friend of mine at the time, replied, "Oh yes, I know her very well."

The woman moved closer. "But, do you know the original Eleanor Schano?"

A bit perplexed, Wendy nodded yes. And then the woman announced in a loud, clear voice, "Well, I can tell you, the Eleanor Schano on TV now is not the first one. Eleanor Schano is like Betty Crocker — they've had lots of them."

I love a good urban legend, but let me go on record here to say there is nothing Betty Crocker-esque about my career. It has always been me, one woman: Eleanor Schano.

If my name sounds familiar it's because I've been out there in the very public arena of the media for a very long time. If my face looks familiar it's because you have welcomed me into your homes for decades reporting the news on television.

If some viewers thought Eleanor Schano was a manufactured character, an identity assigned to different performers over time, I can only assume that it's because I've been on television for so long that I functioned as a veritable walking anthology of hairstyles and fashion over the decades! Blonde, brunette, box jackets and pill box hats, bell bottoms to power suits — you name it, I've tried it on air. And in addition to my looks changing, my broadcast venues changed over the years, too. I've been on every local station in Pittsburgh, and even some of the radio stations. If people assumed there was more than one of me, I can only respond by saying that it's been such a hectic and busy

Prologue

ride that sometimes I wished I could hire a stand-in or two, to help take the heat off!

But that never happened. It's always been me.

People have commented — not unkindly, more in amazement, it seems — that it's hard to believe one person could be on the air for so many years, still standing, let alone walking and talking! But I have been on the air, and though the hairstyles and fashion choices may have changed, my one true goal never wavered: To tell a story, and tell it well.

Throughout the decades, people often said to me, "With the life you've led, you ought'a write a book!" But telling the real story of my life is something I never thought I could do until now, as I sit at the top of the proverbial mountain with a 360 degree panoramic view of how life was back then and how it is now.

Since clearly I am a woman who was not born yesterday, the book you have in your hands is full of history — personal history and the TV industry's history. And to a person who has been on the air fifty-two weeks a year, for the past fifty-two years, those two histories crossed paths a lot!

I have been reporting the news through eleven US presidents, through the space race, Civil Rights, Watergate, and the assassinations of JFK and Martin Luther King, Jr. I was reporting when Neil Armstrong took his first steps on the moon, and when the Beatles took the stage on the Ed Sullivan Show. I was reporting through the rise of the Internet and the fall of the Berlin Wall. I was reporting when Rosa Parks refused to give up her seat on an Alabama bus, and I was reporting when Ms. Parks was laid to rest in a Detroit cemetery at the age of 92.

But "reporter" isn't my only role. In all those years, at the same time that I was a reporter, I went from teen to adult, from daughter to wife, from wife to mother. I went from devoted spouse to divorcee, from divorcee to wife again, and then to widow. I have buried a child, celebrated the lives of my remaining daughters, gone from parent to grandparent, been cared for by my parents, and taken on the role of caretaker for them.

And the plain fact is, it's tough to grow up in front of the camera. It's even tougher to grow old in front of it.

So the decision to recall my life, and commit it to print, is the most difficult journey I have ever undertaken. It's required me to reveal my own true voice, which is an unusual habit for a broadcaster, because we're used to reporting on the lives of others. But hindsight, as they say, is 20/20, and I finally realized that what I've lived through personally and what I've been reporting on professionally for over fifty years aren't so far apart. The lessons I've learned can be lessons to help other people, too.

And so I started to write.

This book has required me to speak from the heart about my own childhood dreams, love, loss, liberation . . . about life's lessons learned from a career as a broadcast journalist battling gender bias, discrimination, and sexual harassment . . . about meeting celebrities and heads of state, and simple people with humble dreams. . . about those moments in life we celebrate; and yes, even those moments we'd rather sweep under the carpet and have everyone else forget!

The most important thing is that the moments are there. Lived and appreciated, for better or worse, these are the moments that made my life my own.

If you were around to witness some of them, I'm glad you've come back to share the memories. If you're meeting me for the first time through these pages, then I welcome you along for the ride, and appreciate your faith in seeing this little sliver of history through my eyes.

1973

PGH'S FIRST FEMALE ANCHORPERSON

Eleanor Schano has won her own battle for equal rights. For twenty-four years she has fought for a place in the male dominated world of news reporting. It was once the policy to give women reporters stories that dealt with flower shows and garden clubs. Eleanor Schano refused to be satisfied with second-rate stories instead, she covered stories that were only given to the men. Ms. Schano's coverage has won her many awards and the respect of everyone in her profession. Eleanor Schano is a pioneer in the field of women's equality and the field of broadcast journalism.

1
Television History 101: How TV and I Came Of Age Together

My first audition was at the WDTV studios in 1951. Located in Pittsburgh's grand Chamber of Commerce building on Seventh Avenue, WDTV consisted of one big room with the "studio" and "control room" separated by a piece of glass. A small adjacent booth held a microphone from which announcers did live voice-over narrations.

The audition was for a series of fashion commercials — and since the audition notice said *"must have TV experience"* only a few people turned up. If anyone had TV experience back in 1951 it must have been from life on another planet.

Television was a brand new industry back then and those getting it off the ground were doing it in the spirit of our pioneers in the old West. I didn't look much like a pioneer at that audition, though: Still a teenager, with my neatly styled hair and proper little high heeled shoes. But I'd been modeling for awhile

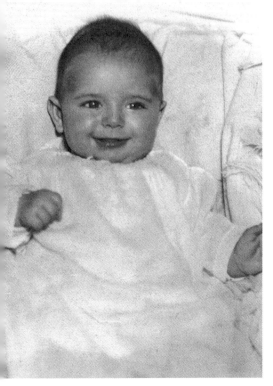

▲ Eleanor at three months . . .

▼ Eleanor ar age six

▲ Eleanor at age two

▼ Grandpap Daley, Eleanor, Mom, Grandma Daley at family farm in Paw Paw, WV

through high school so I figured I could count myself among the "experienced pros."

None of us knew where to stand or where to look when the red camera tally light came on, and the floor manager wasn't that experienced either so his cues were either too late or too early, resulting in a lot of audition*ees* looking like deer in the headlights, and then suddenly breaking into bright grins when we thought we were "on."

Imagine my shock — followed by a delicious thrill — when I got the call saying I was hired, and had to make my live TV debut at WDTV the very next day!

Imagine my shock — followed by the stinging let-down— when I showed up to find out the normal procedure for a live commercial was for the model — *me* — to appear on camera while an announcer described what I was wearing. There I stood, pointing to a Peter Pan collar and twirling around to show off a dirndl skirt and feeling more than a little silly as a male announcer read fashion notes from a script.

It didn't take me long to decide that I could do the narration better. (So what if I had never spoken a word on television!) I left the studio and walked right over to the Frick Building, and up to the eleventh floor to the Jay Reich Agency.

When I told the pleasant-looking receptionist that I wanted to see Mr. Reich, she asked me what it was in regards to. Nerves changed my usual deep voice to a goofy falsetto as I blurted out, "My name is Eleanor Schano and I need to see Mr. Reich right now about a very important matter."

Heaven only knows what she was thinking — a young girl demanding to see this much older man over a "very important matter" — so when she pressed for details I clarified, "It's about his television commercials that I'm doing and I think he's making a big mistake."

That did the trick. Before I knew it, I was ushered right into the biggest office I had ever seen, staring at a very distinguished man seated behind a mahogany desk. He was puffing on a pipe and he asked, in a booming but friendly voice, "Miss Schano, what can I do for you?"

Adrenaline took over and all in one breath I told him, "I just did a commercial for your client and if you really want to sell these things you would let *me* talk about them. Why have the man in the booth describe what I'm wearing while I'm just standing there pointing and feeling silly? If you let *me* talk, I know I can sell lots of stuff for your client."

Jay Reich puffed on his pipe a few moments longer, then said, "You know, that's a good idea."

This great display of moxy got me my very first speaking role . . . *and* an acute panic attack! I left that office with my script in hand, and spent the next twenty-four hours in a deep state of terror. I would be *the very first woman* ever to speak a word on live TV in Pittsburgh! There were many, many ways I could mess it up, and I spent the night imagining every last one of them in painful detail.

But I had no choice. I had to go through with it, so I showed up the next morning at the WDTV studios and changed into the outfit I had to model and describe, all the while running my lines over and over in my head. The floor manager showed me where to stand, sheer dread consumed me, and all too soon he was starting the count-down to my broadcast speaking debut.

Five. . .

What if I freeze in front of the camera?

Four. . .

What if I forget my lines?

Three . . .

What if I'm terrible?

Two . . .

What if I fall in love with this and want to do it for the rest of my life?

You're on.

I never dreamed of becoming a television broadcaster for one very good reason: When I was a kid, there was no television.

I do, however, remember the first time my own written words garnered some attention. I was six years old, in first grade at St. Margaret's school in Greentree, a close suburb of Pittsburgh, Pennsylvania, and I won a poetry contest.

Tiny little snowflakes falling down to earth….
Trying to arrive in time for Our Lord's birth….

That display of poetic spirituality made a big impression on Sister Gonzaga, who subsequently chose me to emcee the Christmas play. The fact that I also was the tallest and had the deepest voice of any boy or girl in the class probably helped, too.

It was my big moment.

How proud I felt standing on the makeshift stage in my navy blue jumper and ugly brown tie shoes. My little heart was beating so fast as the parents began filing into the room, seeing my own Mom and Dad being ushered into the second row.

And that was the beginning. A performer was born — a chubby little girl who wasn't afraid to speak in public, setting her sights on Something Big.

That little performer continued to hone her creative skills — and subject her whole family to them regularly! I loved to put on plays and any time more than two relatives gathered for a visit I staged a production, or insisted on reading poems I had written. For as long as I can remember, I was happiest when I was either writing or talking.

But my dream was not to be a performer professionally. My earliest career aspiration was to be a lawyer — a dream that died young when I proudly announced my plans at a family gathering the Thanksgiving I was ten years old. Uncle Jim was the kind of guy who never said much but when he did he had the sort of self-

WELCOME
OLLYWOOD STARS

Eleanor, left,
with
Hollywood
stars at the
dedication of
old Greater Pittsburgh
International Airport in 1952.
A mural-sized reproduction of
this photo currently hangs at the
Greater Pittsburgh Airport.

appointed authority that left no room for argument. His expression suggested that he was in possession of either great knowledge or acute gas pain. And he liked to talk about cars. (The guy drove an Nash. Doesn't that say something?!)

So there the whole family sat around the dining room table, eating the usual Thanksgiving trimmings, when a lull fell in the adult conversation. Uncle Jim swung his gaze around to me and asked, "Well, little Eleanor, what do *you* want to be when you grow up?" (I was "little" Eleanor, so as not to be confused with my mom of the same name.)

Uncle Jim's demeanor intimidated me but I finally told him, "I want to be a lawyer."

Uncle Jim looked stunned. "Why, little Eleanor," he scoffed, "don't you know you can't be a lawyer?"

This was news to me. "Why not?"

He didn't bother to answer me. Instead, in that same incredulous tone, he addressed his next sentence to the adults at the table. "What's the matter with her? Doesn't little Eleanor understand girls can't be lawyers?"

There was a dead silence. I sat there waiting for someone to contradict him but no one said a word. And that crushed me. I might sound like a Pollyanna when I tell you that up to that point, I could envision myself standing straight and tall in a courtroom, fighting for people's rights. I even pictured how I'd be dressed — in a dark blue suit with a white collared blouse and high heeled pumps.

Since no one bothered to correct Uncle Jim's declaration I just assumed he was right and sadly figured I'd have to choose a new career path. I settled on a new favorite game: Girl Reporter.

It's an idea I got from reading Brenda Starr in the comics. Daddy's yellow flashlight was my microphone and I used it to interview my neighborhood pals. I would make them sit in a circle and one by one I asked them questions like, "Who is your favorite parent?" "Who do you like best, your little brother or big sister?" "What's your favorite vegetable?"

I may not have realized it back then, but I was honing the single most important trait of all news reporters: insatiable curiosity. Some people might call it a genetic flaw but it's one all reporters have in common.

But my childhood wasn't just Brenda Starr and Twenty Questions. I was born in July of 1932, the first-born child in a middle-income family. Along with my younger brother Bob and sister Clare (all of us neatly spaced four years apart), we grew up in Greentree, amidst a few paved roads and a tiny shopping district that included a grocery store, Curly's Ice Cream Shoppe, and a pharmacy owned by someone named (no kidding) Doc Moore. Our family car was a DeSoto, and the gasoline station on the corner had great giveaways with each gallon of gas— including whole ripe watermelons in the summer.

If you weren't making up your own games to play in Johnny Wilson Park, your entertainment came from the radio. We owned a Motorola floor model with a cabinet that resembled a piece of furniture. Everyone listened to the radio back then, for the soaps, for the news, for the music. I curled up next to that radio every day after school, imagining what *Ma Perkins* looked like, envisioning all the characters on *Portia Faces Life* and then *When a Girl Marries*. After the soaps, my little brother Bob moved in for the real excitement: *Tom Mix, Jack Armstrong — All American Boy*, and later in the evening, *The Green Hornet*.

I *loved* the radio, its drama, its beauty, its energy. The only time the radio actually got turned off in my house was during dinnertime, since the news was always about bad things like crime and of course, later on, the big war. But after dinner, it was flipped on again and we all gathered around to listen to George Burns and Gracie Allen, Jack Benny, or Fibber McGee and Molly.

So it's odd that dinnertime — that rare stretch of time spent *without* the radio playing — probably had more influence on my career in broadcasting than any time spent listening to the radio itself. And that's because of my parents.

I was blessed with two very intelligent parents, Joseph and Eleanor Martha Schano, who discussed current events around the dinner table nightly. They also encouraged all of us to read the newspaper every day. Given the fact that there was such an age difference between my brother and sister and me, I really was the only one old enough to engage in my parents' spirited discussions.

And I *wanted* to engage! I pored over the morning *Post-Gazette*; analyzed the afternoon editions of the *Pittsburgh Press* and *Sun Telegraph*. By dinnertime I was ready and waiting to "report" the big stories of the day to mom and dad.

Especially my dad. I adored both of my parents but I had a deep need to "impress" my father. It's something I've come to think of as "dancing for daddy," because I would, throughout my life, crave his approval, and look for that satisfied nod or smile that told me he was proud.

If dad contributed to my "nose for news," then it was my mother who made sure I recited that news perfectly. She was the best speech teacher I could have hoped for. Good grammar was instilled in us. Not one word of slang was permitted in our home and I don't even remember my mother ever once raising her voice! She was a "lady" in every sense of the word, a woman of such grace and dignity and refinement that I wanted to live up to her expectations and live by the example that she set.

So there I was, a teenager in the late 1940's, rather awkward and a loner at school, but able to speak like a professional orator and devour newspapers all day long so I could impress my dad at dinnertime.

With that foundation, I guess it was inevitable that I would react the way I did when I picked up the *Pittsburgh Press* one day and read this headline: *First Television Station Here Soon.*

The year was 1948, and I was just fifteen years old, but my heart stopped and I read that article again and again, documenting the construction of a 500-foot tower on the North Side that would bring television to Pittsburgh by the fall.

It was being built for the Allen DuMont Laboratories, holder of the only TV permit issued for operation in the Pittsburgh market. Operating on Channel 3, 60 to 66 megacycles, the station's call letters would be WDTV. When completed this would mean that Pittsburghers with television sets would be able to receive broadcasts from New York, Philadelphia, Boston and other Eastern cities.

We didn't have a TV set, and when I asked my dad if he thought TV would ever be as popular as radio, he said no. *"People will never sit still staring at a little box in their living room."*

Despite Daddy's opinion, I was relentless in my search to see television, not sure what to expect from this new medium but certain in my heart that this was the beginning of a brand new era. I begged Daddy to take me to see a television, and the only one he knew of was displayed in the window of a neighborhood hardware store. Daddy and I trudged down there on January 11, 1949. It was a frigid, snowy night, and we stood on the sidewalk, peering through the store's window at a 10-inch television set. It was hard to distinguish between the snow falling outside and the snow on the fuzzy TV screen.

At precisely 8:30 p.m., the test pattern was replaced with a slide that said "DuMont Presents Your Magic Window." The broadcast originated from the Syria Mosque (a grand old auditorium that's since been demolished), in the Oakland section of town, with KDKA radio announcer Ed Shaughnessy dressed as a character named Pa Pitt, Pittsburgh Mayor David L. Lawrence, and Dr. Allen B. DuMont himself on hand to present him with a cathode-ray tube.

The program was billed as "The Golden Spike," because with the sign-on of DuMont's WDTV, East and Midwestern cities were finally connected. The coaxial cable that fed programs from one region to another had not yet been completed, so prior to WDTV in Pittsburgh, Midwestern stations that wanted to carry programs from New York City could not air them "live," and had to rely on the inferior quality of kinescope recordings to show later.

On that evening in 1949, WDTV broadcast a variety of local acts, and then at 9:30, all four existing networks showed the "Golden Spike" ceremony, and then each network showed a sample of its programming. Pittsburgh's WDTV signed off after its first night of broadcasting at 11:00 pm.

There were fewer than 4,000 TV sets in Pittsburgh at the time, so few people viewed that inaugural broadcast, but my dad and I watched it all. I scarcely recall breathing and my heart was pounding throughout, and I knew, standing there in the freezing, snowy street in front of the hardware store with my Dad, I just *knew* I was watching history being made.

***

I was so determined to get my foot in the door of broadcasting that I took the only path I could find. I decided maybe I could *model* my way into this emerging industry. I already had *some* modeling experience from high school so I wasn't starting from scratch. At the age of fifteen, I was invited to serve on the Gimbels Department Store High School Fashion Board. It was a prestigious position to sit on Saturday mornings with representatives of other high schools in the region and to meet with esteemed Francene Blum — a short, stocky woman with a knockout sense of style that compensated for her sharp features and severe haircut.

Francene Blum always wore a hat angled over her high forehead, a detail that has stuck in my mind all these years because it seemed to lend her great authority. When Francene Blum spoke, everyone listened! She didn't hesitate to criticize a young woman who arrived to her meeting in bobby sox and saddle shoes. She expected that we dress like fashion models. I think my mother's years of modeling exemplary etiquette paid off for me, because Francene Blum decided I met her high expectations and she took me under her wing by booking me in most of Gimbels' fashion shows. I must admit I was quite impressed with myself and invited all of my relatives to come downtown and "see me model."

Eventually, my modeling career expanded, as I was asked to do runway shows for not only Gimbels but also Hornes, Jonassons, Rosenbaums, Frank & Seder, and Kaufmanns. My face appeared daily on the fashion pages of the *Pittsburgh Press*, *Sun Telegraph* and *Post Gazette*. At one point the *Post-Gazette* even ran a full-page spread dubbing me the city's top model! I was having the time of my life . . . inhaling rarified air and loving every breath.

But make no mistake: My goal was not to pursue modeling as a profession; only to use it to pave my way into a television career. It did not dawn on me that perhaps television was already evolving into a place that wasn't interested in women *unless* they were models.

But I got my first taste of that fact — a message I would hear many, many more times throughout my career — when I was chosen as a local model for Republic Studios'

launch of a big Hollywood movie called *Kon Tiki*. It was about a man who sailed a homemade raft across the Atlantic, and a bunch of Hollywood bigwigs landed in Pittsburgh for a promotional junket. The two stars of the movie were there too and I was chosen to escort them around town.

That's right: I was Miss Kon Tiki.

On the list of public appearances, we were invited to join the dignitaries at the grand opening of the Greater Pittsburgh Airport in 1952. (In fact, if you happen to be passing through the *new* Pittsburgh International Airport, you may notice a huge overhead photo of that historic day, and the tall blonde on the left is me.) It was a whirlwind three-day tour and things were going well until the final day. Before wrapping up the event, the rotund, balding, cigar-smoking movie mogul said he would like to speak to me — in his office above the Art Cinema movie theater on Liberty Avenue.

I eagerly hoped this was the big break I'd been waiting for, but something just didn't feel right as I walked into a shabby, dimly lit room. Mr. Movie Mogul escorted me to a chair across from his desk then pulled out a book of photographs — all young starlets he claimed he'd launched to stardom.

"I arranged for their screen tests, and honey, I can do the same thing for you," he told me as he reached out and grabbed my arm.

I may have been young but I wasn't stupid. It took less than ten seconds for me to understand what was going on and so — in a dramatic gesture that would have worked well on the silver screen — I jumped up and landed the backside of my hand right across his porky little cheek before spinning on my heels and heading for the door.

"Why, Miss Schano," he said nastily as I departed, "did you really think I was going to do all that for you without you doing a little something for me?"

Lesson Number One Learned The Hard Way: *That* is what people are referring to when they snicker about the 'Hollywood Casting Couch.'

So shortly thereafter when another opportunity for stardom loomed — this time on Broadway — I approached it with a lot more caution.

A local business tycoon was backing a Broadway musical called *Wish You Were Here*. I met this man at a press party and it wasn't long before he was cozying up to me and asking if I would like to audition for the chorus line in the show.

"I don't sing or dance," I told him politely.

"Oh, that doesn't matter," he shrugged. "You can just mouth the words to the songs and you'll look pretty in the ensemble." He went on to describe the play in minute detail, right down to the costumes I would wear. "Auditions will be held a week from Wednesday and if you are interested I'll pay your airfare and make a reservation for you at the Plaza Hotel." Of course, *he* would personally escort me to the theater to meet the producer and director.

I told him I would consider it, but what I really meant was, I had to ask my parents. I may have been leery, but I *did* desperately want a career in broadcasting and I thought, *What if this one does turn out to be legitimate*? (Remember, I was *very* young!) I hated to pass on a big opportunity and so I begged my parents to let me go. You can imagine the reaction it got from mom and dad when I told them about this kindly benefactor who had so graciously invited to pay my way to New York and squire me around while I was there!

In the end, my parents relented, on *one* condition: Mom would go with me.

Fine by me, I thought, although I didn't think that one teensy-weensy detail was something the "kindly benefactor" needed to know.

True to his word, the guy sent me a plane ticket to NYC, along with a note asking me to meet him in the Palm Room at the Plaza Hotel. Mom paid her own airfare, and the two of us arrived to a beautiful hotel room with rich ruby red brocade drapes and a bathroom with a marble vanity. I was living large and feeling oh-so-grown-up as I changed into my pretty brown and white houndstooth suit, and at six o'clock sharp mom and I stepped off the elevator and into the Palm Room.

As long as I live, I will never forget the look on my would-be sugar daddy's face when I introduced him to my mom!

"Thank you for the lovely accommodations," my mother said with a smile.

He looked like he'd just swallowed a bug! He gulped down his drink, gave mom and me the tickets to the musical, then quickly went on his way. I never saw or heard from him again.

Okay, so maybe Broadway wasn't going to pave my way into broadcasting . . . but it *did* teach me a valuable lesson: I aspired to work in an industry that very clearly separated the broadcasters from the broads.

Television may have been in its infancy but it was a *boy* baby and the proud papas who dominated the industry would hire only men to fill the key positions. If they needed an announcer, they looked to radio, which was, no surprise, also dominated by men. We were okay as models, and as starlets and chorus girls and as a pretty decoration on a guy's arm.

But as reporters? *Uh-uh!*

I guess they were able to make enough room for me — the pretty little girl fresh out of her teens — because while I may have been speaking on television, it was only to twirl a skirt and talk about female fashions. Looking back, I think most of the men considered me to be a kind of cute mascot.

Instead of crushing my dreams it only added to my determination. By the time I hit twenty, I *knew* this was where I wanted to be. And for the men who were just keeping me around as "eye candy," well . . . they'd find out soon enough that this "mascot" had a mind of her own!

Modeling early days

2
Pioneering in the Public Eye

*A*s the model and narrator of those early fashion commercials — the ones I so boldly declared *I* should voice instead of the usual male announcer — I had my foot in the door, and it gave me a good reason to hang around as much as possible to see how the rest of the operation was run.

The "rest of the operation," at this point, meant *The Pitt Parade*. It was a 10-minute newsreel that ran before signoff on WDTV each weeknight at 10:00 p.m., right after the last network show — and it was in *that* program that my fashion commercials ran.

The Pitt Parade came about in an interesting way. There was a huge problem when it came time to put that inaugural Golden Spike television program together back in 1949 — the one dad and I had watched through the window of the neighborhood hardware store. *Someone* had to write the script and produce the show, and there were few production companies in the city of

Pittsburgh at the time. One of them was Packaged Programs, which began in the early 1940's when two men named Bill Beale and Morrey Fierst started producing radio shows. Bill Beale offered to take on the job of producing the Golden Spike program, but with one provision: In return, *Packaged Programs* would get free air time on the fledgling WDTV. Bill's idea was to produce a nightly newsreel that would become *The Pitt Parade*.

Since WDTV had no local programming and since the deal wouldn't cost the station a dime, DuMont agreed, and Packaged Programs sent out photographers armed with 16mm film cameras to record the city's events of the day. It was only two days after WDTV went on the air that *The Pitt Parade* made its debut.

Packaged Programs produced *Pitt Parade* out of a cramped third-floor space on Penn Avenue. The reception area doubled as an office space for the other constant presence — and my personal hero — Dan Mallinger.

He was a strong powerful looking man with wide shoulders and a heavy, square jaw — usually with a pipe clenched between his teeth — and spectacles enhancing his perceptive expression. His face was terribly serious and often he lapsed into a thinking pause, hands clasped under his chin. His eyes blinked rarely and I could tell when he was struggling for the right words — he sucked in his upper lip.

If Dan was a good writer, his delivery was even better. He wrote and narrated the scripts for *Pitt Parade* and he had one of the best voices in the business. I loved to watch and listen. The incessant din of the typewriter captured my imagination.

Some day I will be writing news scripts just like Dan, I thought.

I'd been hanging around *Packaged Programs* for months, even when I had no real reason to be there, not only soaking in the atmosphere that I loved, but also silently observing and listening and waiting for an opening. Often there were tight deadlines and one afternoon things were really out of control. Too many stories to write — too little time. This was it — the chance I'd been waiting for. I jumped up and grabbed a pad of scribbled notes and indicated with a nod that I could write a couple of scripts. I wanted the offer to sound confident yet casual, but inside, my heart was pounding.

Dan barely paused, just gave me the nod and went back to work, and with my insides dancing and outside composed, I sat down to type. On the whole, Dan must have been satisfied. He used my copy without one edit, and *that* is about the hugest compliment a broadcast writer can get!

After that day, Dan Mallinger gave me all of the "kickers" to write. A kicker is the term used for the feature at the very end of a newscast. These stories are usually either humorous little slices of life, or boring tidbits that helped fill the time. Kickers may be short, but they present a huge challenge: Try to make a dog show or parade sound compelling.

But I labored away at it, grateful to be writing anything at all for a real newscast, even though I'd still cast longing glances at Dan as he covered the "hard" news, such as politics and police reports.

I also still was doing the fashion commercials for which I'd originally been hired. In fact, that role soon expanded, as Packaged Programs asked me to *produce* some of the new fashion commercials they'd been hired to do. Since television was so new, only a handful of local people knew how to produce commercials. And, of course, there was always a crush of work and too few people to get it all done. Those factors worked in my favor. Since I was already doing the modeling and narration for the fashions, I'm sure Bill Beale offered me that opportunity to produce as much for the sake of convenience as out of any show of confidence.

Cameraman Fred DiFiore and I learned "on-the-job," as the two of us were sent on-location at The Nola Shops to shoot a :30 commercial spot. We were gone for *hours* and the two of us came back with enough footage to fill a 30-minute program! We learned a valuable lesson that day: The more you shot, the more

Student Model Proves Beauty, Brains Mix

One look at Eleanor Schano, Arts freshman, and the firmest believers that beauty and brains don't mix, will change their minds.

The brown-eyed beauty doubles as a professional model and a full-time student. Her modeling requires that she work 30 hours weekly which gives her very little leisure time after her studies are completed.

A television fashion show is Eleanor's aim. She hopes that the training she will receive in radio journalism at Duquesne will aid her in this aim.

WDTV, local television station, is not unfamiliar to this lovely miss. She has advertised for many dealers on several television shows and was a regular member of a popular Wednesday night quiz program.

Star Model

The downtown department stores claim Eleanor as a star model in almost all of their numerous fashion shows. Posing for local newspaper photographers is another of her many occupations in the modeling field.

At present she is the favorite model of an outstanding Pittsburgh commercial photographer, who teaches photography classes at Tech.

Schooling

After graduating from Dormont high school, Eleanor attended Barry College in Florida for a short time, and did part-time modeling in Miami. She has chosen to remain in Pittsburgh throughout the year so that she may continue her schooling during the summer months.

Eleanor has already put her best foot forward in a successful modeling career and can hardly miss becoming a well-known Pittsburgh personality.

Eleanor Schano models a coat dress of suede fabric, one of fashions latest dictates.

you had to slog through to decide what to edit, and it took us a long time to come up with that first commercial.

We got a lot better after that; in fact, Fred and I worked quite well as a team. Since *Pitt Parade* aired every night and since there were two commercial spots in each episode, we had to produce ten commercials a week. It was a crazy, busy time for me, because in addition to my work both on camera and behind-the-scenes, I had started college at Duquesne University in Pittsburgh. Right after graduating from high school, I had spent a year at Barry College in Miami, majoring in business, but I'd come back to Pittsburgh because of a very handsome young man I'd met on holiday break. (That relationship didn't work out, but I guess you could call it Divine Intervention because it's what got me back to Pittsburgh at just the right time to launch my television career!) So now I was a sophomore at Duquesne, business major discarded in favor of a journalism major, and splitting my days between the work I did at *Packaged Programs* for air on WDTV, and the usual college classes and exams.

One client, Robert Hall Clothing, purchased a series of 24 *live* commercials a week, which meant I would have to be at the studio for a 9 am spot . . . rush up to the Duquesne campus for class . . . race back down to the studio for another commercial at noon. . . head back up to class . . . head back to the studio for the 2 pm spot . . . and back there again for the final two commercials during the 6 pm *Buzz-n-Bill Show.*

Frankly, I loved it.

People would stop me on the street and ask if I was "that girl from television." My fellow journalism majors at Duquesne (mostly male) looked at me as a quaint little oddity, and I'd say I was basically a loner on campus. But when it came to my *other* life in production, I was one of the crowd. Maybe I was the sole "girl" on the outermost fringes of the crowd, but a part of the crowd nonetheless.

Being the "girl in the crowd" also meant I got asked out on dates. *A lot.*

I still lived at home because, according to my father, no respectable young unmarried woman would dare live alone. (Remember, we're talking about the early 1950's!) And even though I was 21, dad still insisted on a curfew. Most nights I was home right on time. There *was* one exception, though, and it was grand enough to attract the attention of the entire neighborhood!

Bill Brant was a radio disc jockey turned TV show host. He was a superstar in the area and a hero of mine. I'd listened to him on the radio as a young girl! So when Bill invited me and my boyfriend-of-the-moment to accompany him and his wife on an evening boat excursion, I was over-the-moon! What an honor! What *proof* that I was counted among the broadcast elite!

Very full of myself, I climbed aboard Bill Brant's boat and off we sailed . . . right over a dam! I guess you could say Bill's navigational skills weren't all that well-honed. No one was hurt, but we were, literally, *up the creek without a paddle.* It got late, the fog rolled in, and there we all sat, with the motor idling until daybreak, and me *very, very* late for my curfew!

You can guess the rest of the story. Dad called the police, a search got underway, and when I finally got home the next morning I was met by a police squad car and my father out in the street wearing a white terrycloth bathrobe, with its huge hole in the back revealing Dad's dislike for underwear!

Dad kept pretty close tabs on me and my dates after that. My television career didn't impress my father, to tell you the truth. Not that he *disapproved.* I just think because women in our family did not have careers, Dad didn't wonder *what* I was doing so much as *why* I was doing it. My mom, on the other hand, was my biggest supporter, and my biggest fan. She thought everything I did was great and she offered constructive criticism and tried very hard never to miss one of my TV appearances.

Still, I wonder if they both expected my fascination with broadcasting to be a "phase" I'd outgrow once I met a man and got married.

Because I lived at home, Mom and Dad were aware of any dates I had, and any relationships that blossomed. After the great Bill Brant boating incident, the next man I started dating was a popular disc jockey who worked at WJAS radio. WJAS was in the Chamber of Commerce Building, the same as WDTV, so we bumped into each other often. His name was Barry Kaye, and since this was in the days of "payola" — when disc jockeys were courted by record companies to spin their top tunes — Barry always had an invitation to attend one big event or another. He asked me to join him and so for awhile, there I was, on Barry's arm being wined and dined by the biggest stars on the planet at the time! You name them: Sammy Davis, Jr., Vic Damone, Harry Belefonte. . . they all came through Pittsburgh and I was sitting ringside.

And then one day Dad asked me a question I wasn't prepared to answer.

"Eleanor, is Barry Jewish?"

I didn't even understand the question. My life had been very sheltered, I realized. When I was very young, I thought people only fell into two categories: Catholics, who attended the Catholic school, or Publicans, who attended public school. Talk about naïve!

I sort of stammered, "I don't know if he's Jewish, Dad. I'll ask him."

And I did. Later that night, we were driving downtown in Barry's blue Cadillac convertible, on our way to opening night of the Four Lads at Lenny Litman's Copa.

"Hey, Barry, my dad wants to know if you're Jewish," I said casually.

Barry looked at me like I was a little nuts. "Yeah, of course I'm Jewish."

Trust me when I tell you that at that time I had no idea any kind of race or religious discrimination existed. I was totally shocked to learn that this kind of thing could make a difference to anyone — and certainly not in my own family!

But it *did* make a difference. In fact, my Grandma didn't say it in so many words, but she implied that it would kill her if I married a Jewish boy. My parents met the news with tight-lipped stares that spoke volumes louder than any words.

Looking back, I am ashamed of their prejudices, although I do understand that they were a product of a generation that cared a lot more about "what people think" than "how people feel." My parents held many strong beliefs and one of them was that a Catholic woman would only create problems by marrying a Jewish man.

Remember what I said about "dancing for daddy?" Well, this was the biggest crisis I'd encountered to date in that arena, and in the end, I decided to dance once again for my dad. I broke it off with Barry Kaye.

To my relief, Barry didn't mourn the break-up for long. In fact, almost immediately, he went off on vacation at Grossinger's in the Catskills, where he met a Jewish girl whom he married after a whirlwind two-day courtship!

With this experience raw in my mind, the next time I accepted a date it was with a television director at WDTV. His name was Warren Dana, a nice Catholic boy from a good family, with a Masters Degree and a decent job. Mom and Dad were thrilled that I had finally "come to my senses."

Warren and I dated for the next two years, and maybe it wasn't in the front row at the Copa, but they were nice dates, companionable and easy. Like many young women of my time lacking serious romantic experience, I was "in love with being in love." And it was easy to be in love with Warren Dana. He was good-looking, my parents approved, and since Warren also worked in broadcasting, he accepted my burgeoning television career, wasn't impressed by any so-called "celebrity status," plus he understood the hectic nature of my schedule. We seemed like the perfect match.

Much to my parents' surprise, though, that deepening romantic relationship didn't distract me from my desire to work in broadcasting. If anything, at that point in time I'd say I was more determined than ever! Television had come into its own in the early 1950's, and every day was a fly-by-the-seat-of-your-pants experience filled with energy, and a buzz in the atmosphere. I loved it, and kept showing up day after day filled with a thrill that I was part of it all. My favorite thing was the little news set that amounted to no more than a curtain and a desk, but which, in my mind, was an acclaimed and hallowed place that symbolized my deepest aspirations. I wanted to sit there, I wanted to deliver the news. In the meantime, I'd keep delivering the fashion commercials.

Those of us who were on-air were referred to as "talent," although I think the only real talent we possessed was being able to look into the red tally light of a camera and connect with the viewer. It was just something you had to feel and I felt it. I loved being "on."

I tried to make a point of being at *Packaged Programs* when the daily assignments were handed out to the photographers. I watched when they came back with the raw footage and put it in the "soup" (the processor) and when they did the editing. It was quick and dirty but it was a newscast, and I wanted to know every single detail about how it was put together. I was proud to have gotten to the place that I was at, but I wanted to be a newscaster, I wanted to be a reporter, I wanted to do the kind of work my hero Dan Mallinger was doing.

With a studio now in full operation, WDTV had started its first live local newscast. Hard to believe but the evening news was only five minutes long back then! Still, it was an important production and to appear on it was a prestigious career move. WDTV did carry some network news from CBS with Douglas Edwards. Later, the Camel News Caravan with John Cameron Swayze proved the incredible power of sponsor identification that existed even back then. It was not unusual for the advertising agency to pick the newscaster, to essentially control the newscast.

The first newsman at WDTV was *Ed Wood for Chevrolet*. Truly, that may as well have been his actual full name, because that's how he was ID'd in every newscast! The newscasters' names became synonymous with their sponsors.

I daydreamed about a newscast featuring *Eleanor Schano for Chevrolet*. What I got was additional commercial modeling contracts. That may not have been the direction I wanted to take but it was a feather in my cap just the same, and ultimately it turned out to be the stepping stone to the next phase of my broadcast career. A client hired me to do twenty live commercials a week, pretty high visibility that caught the eye of the WDTV Program Manager. I was pretty, I was well-spoken. *Voila!* He offered me the job of Weather Girl.

That was the job title: Weather Girl.

This was long before the advent of the TV meteorologist, and doing the weather required no scientific knowledge. There were no bells and whistles, just a simple map of the United States. All I had to do in my role of Weather Girl was smile and point and say a few words about low and high pressure systems as they moved across the country. No need to write, no need to report, as I longed to do. All I needed was a big smile and decent stems.

Prior to my Weather Girl debut, though, the nightly newscast didn't even have a weather segment, so it was a first for me as well as a first for the local television market. And while I may have been the *first* Weather Girl, it's the way many female journalists ultimately broke into the business, including ABC's Diane Sawyer.

If the fashion commercials contributed to the stereotype of a smiling model, then this new role became a complete caricature: The Smiling Weather Girl! Rain or shine, all that really mattered was that I kept smiling. Remember what I said about the advertising agencies controlling the newscast? Well, at one point, a mattress company signed on to sponsor the Saturday night 11 p.m. weather segment, and they suggested it would be cute if

I delivered the weather wearing a negligee. And guess what . . . *I did it!*

Why? First, I was happy to have a full-time job on television. I had worked too hard to get to the position I was at in my career and I wasn't about to give it up. Second, I was in no position to argue with the boss.

So, for the duration of the 13-week mattress company contract, I smiled and I talked about low and high pressure systems while wearing a negligee and lounging across a mattress in front of a map of the United States.

Another time I was chosen for a commercial for a heating company. I was to stand on a set that looked like the inside of a living room and when the camera shifted I had to walk up a flight of steps, all the while delivering my lines about this home being the epitome of fine living. (I pronounced it "epi-tome" at the time.) The sponsor thought it would add a little sizzle to the spot if I wore a short skirt, sheer black stockings, and stiletto heels in this role.

I guess the final joke was on the sponsor because I did wear that get-up but as I started to climb the little mock staircase I teetered on the stiletto heels, and ended up tripping and falling over backwards!

Ahhh, the good ol' days of live TV. . .

It paints quite a picture of how women were viewed back then in the 1950's, though, doesn't it? I began to seriously wonder if things would ever change. Once I lamented that fact to my friend and veteran TV newscaster Dave Murray, and he tried to console me by pointing out how much attention was devoted to selecting someone to do commercials and the weather.

"Put a pretty girl on the tube and people will watch her," was how he explained it.

That wasn't what I wanted to hear. I didn't want to be on "the tube" because I was pretty; I longed to be recognized on "the tube" as a writer and serious newswoman.

Through persistence and the sheer fact of my constant presence, I did manage to parlay the Weather Girl gig into some additional assignments. In every career, I suppose there are moments you'd rather permanently erase from the resumé and my involvement in a show called *Guest to Ghost* is one of them! You know how Vanna White spins letters on *Wheel of Fortune?* I guess you could say that in addition to my many broadcast "firsts" I also pioneered the role of TV Game Show Babe on *Guest to Ghost* — a dubious honor to be sure!

The format of *Guest to Ghost* was pretty dumb. The host would ask questions and if the panelist didn't know the answer, I would place a white sheet over his head. Get it? The "guest" would become a "ghost." And of course, I did it all wearing a lovely skimpy dress.

The host of the show was a radio broadcaster from KQV trying to make the leap to television. His name: Bill Burns. It was not an unusual course for a future broadcast journalist. Walter Cronkite had been host of *The Morning Show* on CBS and Mike Wallace had been host of an NBC quiz show called *The Big Surprise*. Burns himself went on to become one of the most revered newsman in Pittsburgh broadcasting history, but back then he was young and feeling his way around the on-camera position.

Let's just say that for all involved, "dignity" was a lost cause. Staff announcer George Eisenhaurer once described *Guest to Ghost* as "the worst program ever on television." But, since it was heavily sponsored by Rosenbaum's department store, it generated enough revenue to stay on the air for over a year.

By 1954, my on-air status was firmly entrenched. I had appeared on *Guest to Ghost,* I was still working as Weather Girl, I continued producing and appearing in fashion commercials, and I was writing the kicker segments for the news. I also made the occasional appearance on the only other television station in town, WQED.

The first public television station in the nation, WQED sprang to life in April, 1954, when a young and earnest man named Fred Rogers developed a program called *The Children's Corner*, showcasing local singer and performer Josie Carey. WQED was billed as an educational television station, and they supported themselves with donations from viewers. The cornerstone of the station was *The Children's Corner*, though, and the songs and puppet characters introduced there eventually morphed into *Mr. Rogers Neighborhood*, which continued to produce original episodes for the next forty-plus years. Fred Rogers' work and reputation are now — and forever will be — the stuff of legends.

That first year, WQED featured live coverage of the Allegheny County Fair and I had a small role gathering notables and bringing them to the camera. Later, when they started a quiz show called *The Greeks Had A Word For It*, all of the local on-air talent rotated through as guests, and I took my shot at it, too. Infinitely more dignified than *Guest to Ghost*, KDKA radio announcer Jim Westover hosted the show. He'd say a word in Greek and we had to give the English derivative, and as you could guess, there was more humor and entertainment than actual information involved.

Still, I figured all of this on-camera exposure would eventually add up to enough to get me into the role of news reporter, and while I was impatient to see other men getting to that position before me simply by virtue of their gender, I never doubted for an instant that one day it *would* be my turn.

By the end of 1954, WDTV was scheduled to move to the brand new Gateway Center One Building by Point State Park. It was a time that marked Pittsburgh's first renaissance, a period that changed the city's skyline. By then, the DuMont network was facing financial straits, and its only way to obtain cash was to sell WDTV to Westinghouse Electric. It was a $6.75 *million* dollar deal, and while we all were sad to see DuMont gasping its last breath, we looked forward with great anticipation to the move from our cramped quarters on the mezzanine of the Chamber of Commerce building to the pristine studios that awaited us at Gateway Center One.

The life I was leading seemed to be charmed. Just think: I was still in high school when television premiered in Pittsburgh in 1949, and by the end of 1954, here I was, considered a seasoned television veteran!

It was Christmas Eve, 1954, when the final piece of the puzzle fell into place: Warren Dana asked me to marry him. I had discovered television, television had discovered me, and on top of it all I would walk down the aisle with my handsome husband and live happily ever after.

By January 1, 1955, I figured my entire life was in order and that it would continue to be a whirlwind of celebrity status mixed with marital bliss. I could never have predicted what awaited me — both professionally and personally — just around the bend.

●

One Man's Trash Becomes
a Cities Hidden Treasure

*P*itt Parade may have been primitive by today's standards, but it was extremely popular. It stayed on the air for ten years, most of the time as part of a live evening newscast.

Since Packaged Programs owned Pitt Parade, the archives became the property of photographer Fred DiFiore, who had bought the business from longtime partners Bill Beale and Morrey Fierst.

Packaged Programs went out of business in the 1960's and since Fred didn't know what to do with the hundreds of film cans gathering dust in the back room, he hauled them to his own basement — where they continued to sit and gather dust.

Many, many years later, Fred and I crossed paths again at WTAE TV. I was a reporter by then, he was a cameraman, and often we teamed up to cover a story. One day, coming back from an assignment, Fred and I started reminiscing about the old days when the subject of Pitt Parade came up.

Rhetorically, I mused, "I wonder what ever happened to all of that film?"

Fred not only admitted that all those film cans were stashed behind the furnace in his basement but that his wife Alta kept threatening to toss them in the trash!

We cooked up the idea that Fred should approach WTAE and ask if they wanted to buy this historic footage. They turned down the offer and it seemed nothing was going to happen until Alta decided to call the trash collector.

The thought of that historic footage stuck in my mind. What a tragic loss it would be, and so later, while talking to an old friend at KDKA TV, I mentioned this film collection stashed away in Fred's basement. Within 24 hours, KDKA contacted Fred and made a deal to buy the entire Pitt Parade collection. Alta DiFiore reclaimed her basement and KDKA owned a treasure trove of the city's history that never could have been duplicated. It's probably the only station in the country that can boast a ten-year history of its city captured on film during the infancy of television in the early 1950's.

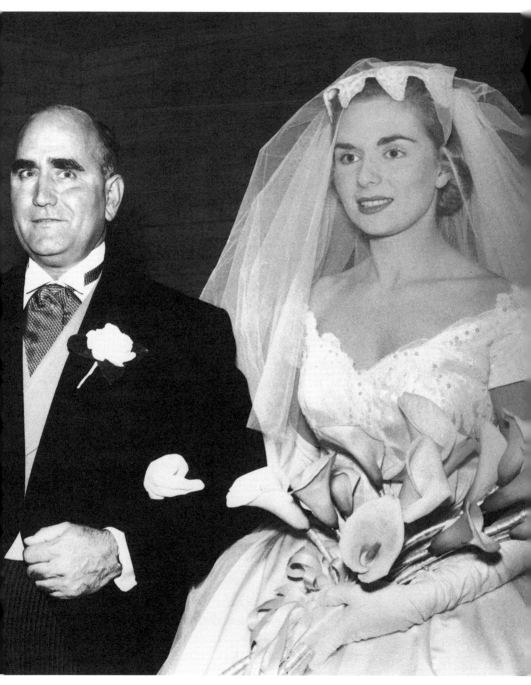

April 30, 1955

3

When Life Intrudes

*L*ife seemed simple in the early 1950's. Even though the networks reported on Korea's being permanently partitioned across the DMV. . . even as the US Senate denounced Joseph McCarthy's "witch hunts" . . . even as Malcolm X came to prominence as the head of the Nation of Islam in New York. . . it all seemed far, far away from life in Pittsburgh.

I was 23 years old and excitedly planning my wedding with the help of my mom. I still lived in my parents' house, where milk was delivered to our back door every morning, the dry-cleaner picked up and delivered our clothes, and a bakery truck dropped off fresh baked bread and sugar donuts.

At work, the news covered politics and some local crime, but overall it seemed like the neighborhoods were safe, kids were allowed to play in the woods and walk in the park, and families consisted of Dads and Moms living together in the same house where they raised their kids. Divorce was a scandal and I didn't know anyone who had personally ever gone through it.

The sale of WDTV to Westinghouse Electric went through, and at Noon precisely on January 31, 1955, the call letters were changed to KDKA-TV and the dial position moved from Channel 3 to Channel 2. It didn't take long for the viewing public to get used to the change. After all, there was only one commercial station in town.

Every day I showed up to work at Gateway Center One, KDKA TV, elated to be working in an honest-to-goodness newsroom and convinced I had the best job in the world. Imagine the scene: News desks, typewriters, wire machines . . . even a "talent lounge" for us on-air performers!

KDKA occupied three floors in Gateway One. The first floor contained a huge studio, designated Studio A, where all of the major programs would originate. The lower level contained the newsroom, production offices, and film editing suites, and the second floor housed the sales department and executive suites. It all added up to the ability to do lavishly produced programs. For the first time, we had a permanent news set, no shabby little desk in front of a lopsided curtain. I eyed that news set at KD with a pounding heart, *certain* this would be the place where I made my news reporter debut.

They were great days. I made friends easily and became one of the crowd that would gather for chicken a la king and Boston crème pie in a little restaurant called the Colonade, located in an underground passageway connecting all of the Gateway buildings. I got used to being the only female in a crowd that included Pittsburgh's broadcast icons, men like Bill Burns, Rege Cordic, Sterling Yates, Carl Ide, Bill Brant and Al McDowell. They treated me like just another colleague, which I was sure indicated that one day soon they'd accept me as a news reporter.

Around town, we were hailed as celebrities.

Never was that fact more apparent than the day of my wedding, April 30, 1955. It was a star-studded event that included heavy press coverage and many dignitaries on the guest list — including the mayor of Pittsburgh, David L. Lawrence! Warren Dana and I exchanged vows during a high mass at St. Margaret's Church in Green Tree, that same little church where I had once gone to grade school.

The weather was all shining and glorious, and sunlight glinted off of my wedding gown, a dazzling white thing mother and I had shopped and shopped for. It was a Priscilla of Boston design with pearl-encrusted satin panels, a scooped neckline, and a long, long train. It was beautiful. . . I just don't know who came up with the idea of taking one of the appliquéd flowers from the satin panel and plunking it on my head like a frilly pancake!

My bridesmaids were my very best friends — mostly gorgeous models — who wore shocking pink chiffon chosen by my little sister Clare. One of Warren's groomsmen was Bill Brant. (Daddy had finally started to speak to him again after that horrific riverboat experience!)

After the Mass, guests attended the reception at the Pittsburgh Athletic Association. My new father-in-law, Peter Dana, was the National Sales Manager for Universal Motion Pictures, so many of the guests were his show business friends. I remember looking over the crowded reception area and thinking there could only be blissful days ahead.

And at first, they were.

Warren and I had worked long enough that we could afford a down-payment on a little house in the Pittsburgh suburb of Scott Township. Those early months were like playing house for me, learning to cook, putting up wallpaper, decorating with lots of imagination and little money, throwing dinner parties for friends.

TV Guide even featured us in a photo spread with the headline "*The Cupid Here Was KDKA-TV!*" We wore matching shirts, and accompanying photos show me whisking something in a pot while Warren — sporting a puffy chef's hat and a puzzled gaze — reads from a cookbook.

The new Mrs. Dana at the end of a long day of putting the finishing touches on their honeymoon house.

The groom, holding a copy of ▶ Good Housekeeping, instructs Eleanor in a few things every wife should know about a lawn.

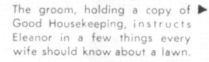

◀ She waits to see what goes into the pot next while a puzzled chief cook and bottle-washer pores over what every husband should know.

Only in the 50's would this "silliness" sell magazines.

TV Guide referred to me as "the new Mrs. Dana," although at work I still went by the name Eleanor Schano. I had worked so hard to create that identity that I wasn't about to give it up. I even put together a proposal to do a program called *Women of the '50's*. In my mind, it was a show that would present provocative interviews and information of substance dealing with the issues that affected women in daily life.

It worked. I got my own show at last. But guess what: The program director decided the only way it would sell advertising time and attract female viewers would be if it was called *The Beauty Spot*. It sounded so frivolous, the polar opposite of what I envisioned, but arguing my case got me nowhere. Determined to make the best of it, I became the host — and producer — of my very first talk show. The program director was a little anxious about the whole endeavor, so he suggested I have an older woman as a co-host.

"It will add a dimension of maturity," he assured me.

What that really meant was "it would lend me credibility." It's a funny concept here in the 21st Century where youth is glorified. Fifty years ago, it was more of a *liability*, and I confess even I lied about my age — telling people I was *older* than I actually was — so my youth wasn't held *against* me.

Ahhh, how times have changed!

But if "maturity" was what they wanted, "maturity" was what they got. Addie Sachs came on board, a lovely lady 20 years my senior, who sat by my side and discussed issues of the day. We'd throw out a topic and then offer up our opinions, covering everything from rock and roll to Rosa Parks.

That format didn't last long, though, as eventually the program director believed I was capable of flying solo. And I loved it! I booked newsmakers of the day, aiming for the women in my city who were making a difference. . . women like Dr. Dorothy Finklor, the founder of Point Park College. She was a remarkable woman who once said during an interview, "I have never been afraid of anything in my life."

I have never forgotten those words, or her conviction and self-confidence as she said them. Her statement stayed with me and inspired me many times over the years.

As *The Beauty Spot* profiled progressive women of the era, I admit I saw myself as among their ranks. I was doing it all, working in an exciting career by day, coming home to my husband and our newlywed home at night. All very fairytale-ish, all very satisfying.

And as the children's ditty goes, *first comes love, then comes marriage* . . . then comes Eleanor with a baby carriage.

Less than a year after my wedding, I was pregnant.

It wasn't planned. I was a good Catholic girl raised to rely on the "rhythm" method — although I guess you could say I never really got into the rhythm of it! Nevertheless, Warren and I were thrilled by the news. We decorated a nursery, put up wallpaper with whimsical pastel balloons and teddy bears, bought a rocking chair, lots of stuffed animals.

Like every mother-to-be, I counted the days until the birth of my baby, although I did continue to work. You couldn't even say the word "pregnant" on air back then, let alone appear that way on TV! But the loose-fitting fashions of the day worked in my favor, and I was able to disguise my "condition" for quite a few months.

When the big day finally arrived, I headed off to the hospital full of hope and excitement. My obstetrician was on staff at a hospital not known for its birthing facilities. The labor suite was so primitive it looked very much like a Girl Scout camp dormitory with six beds lined up against a back wall with only a sheer curtain separating the mothers-to-be. A lump congealed in my throat as I entered the drab room and heard women in various stages of labor screaming in pain. The shrill sound never stopped and eventually I realized I had become one of them.

A short middle aged woman with hair parted down the middle and rolled up neatly on both sides introduced herself as she helped me into a hospital gown and assigned me to the only empty bed. I was in the corner and for the next 12 hours I would lie there alone, frightened and staring at the warped and water-stained ceiling.

I was not prepared for what I was enduring. No one had told me what it would really be like to deliver a baby. Doctors didn't communicate with their patients very much in those days and I was so frightened that I cried until tears just wouldn't come anymore.

It may be commonplace today for husbands, mothers and friends to accompany the expectant mom to the labor suite, but keep in mind that back then, all of those folks sat out in a waiting room, and other than the occasional nurse coming through, expectant moms sweated it out on their own. Finally, through the delirium, I recall the sudden spinning awareness that I was being wheeled into another room. Voices around me indicated my baby was about to enter the world. The lights were blinding and I begged for someone to take the pain away.

It finally did stop and as any mother who has just given birth knows — that beautiful encounter with your newborn makes all the pain and suffering instantly vanish.

My daughter Mary had arrived.

It was July 7, 1956, and while the joy was intense, the moment was short-lived. Even though Mary was a full-term infant, her one little lung had not inflated properly and the doctor ordered that she be put into an incubator to assist her breathing. At the same time, I was sent to my hospital room and confined to bed. I wasn't even permitted to visit the nursery. My little Mary was two days old and I had only seen her for about 30 seconds. The nurses told me to be patient — that she was doing well and by tomorrow she would be in my arms.

That tomorrow never came.

During the early hours of the morning, premature twins were born and a young resident physician made the decision to have my infant removed from the incubator. The nursery only had two units and he said he needed both of them for the twins.

It was a horrible mistake — one that took my baby's life. Mary died within half an hour. I'll never forget the feeling, the reality of living in your worst possible nightmare.

There seemed to be little compassion or understanding of the emptiness and loss I was feeling. Instead of being moved to another floor where babies' cries wouldn't be heard, I was told I had to stay in my room, which was directly across from the nursery. Four times a day I watched from my bed as blue- and pink-clad newborns were delivered to their mothers. I saw balloons and flowers and heard the joyous sounds of new parents and grandparents exclaiming and bragging over their precious little bundles.

Everyone in our family was devastated, completely in shock. My parents grieved and mourned, and I think my grandfather, so looking forward to the honor of becoming a great-grandfather, took the news even harder than they did.

My husband Warren was devastated. But he managed to remain focused in the midst of his grief and took on the terrible task of arranging for Mary's burial. Her tiny body was placed in a casket where it rests today with my grandparents John and Eleanor Daley.

It is now well over forty years since I lost my first child but time has not erased the memory of those days, weeks and months that followed. There was no such thing as grief counseling when my baby Mary died. I would sob — alone — often hoping someone would hear my cries and offer help, comfort, *anything* to take the pain away.

I became obsessed with babies. Every time I walked down a street or joined a crowd of people all I could seem to focus on were the babies. I would walk up to strangers and ask how old their infants were, and would use it as a benchmark to dream about how big my baby would have grown.

All I knew was I wanted Mary back.

My family and friends urged me to return to work and with no real enthusiasm I returned to doing commercials, the weather and *The Beauty Spot* at KDKA-TV.

With only one TV station to watch in Pittsburgh, even the smallest event in the private life of an on-air personality made news. In the best of times it seemed my name appeared weekly in the *Pittsburgh Press* and *TV Guide*, so it was no surprise that the death of my child was reported on as well. And the public responded with an outpouring of sympathy that makes my heart swell to this day. It was overwhelming; thousands of viewers sent notes of condolences, letters to offer kind words and prayers.

That support from viewers made me realize that I had to rise above those personal feelings when I was on air. It gave me a more mature understanding of the responsibilities of a broadcaster: Carry on with a happy face no matter what happened in your private life. I appreciated the viewers' sympathies, but I owed it to them to move forward and get the focus back on the news, not on me. I think any true broadcasting professional understands that rule, and so we manage to cultivate cool and composed public personas, which we can trot out on command.

And so I continued to trot out my public persona for work but inside the spark was extinguished. Broadcasting, which once had been my life's dream, was now nothing more than a way to fill the day. Perhaps with that euphoria gone, I was able to objectively assess my career and realize my role at KDKA-TV would never change. But even *that* didn't bother me. I had lost my spirit and my willingness to fight for what I believed was right.

Around this time, rumors were circulating that a new TV station would be on the air within a year — WIIC TV, which would eventually become WPXI — and it was a rumor that sent just about everyone at KDKA scurrying to update their resumes. Although my colleagues encouraged me to do the same, I didn't

Bus Stop longest run in Pittsburgh Playhouse history starring Eleanor Schano and Gaines Kincaid.

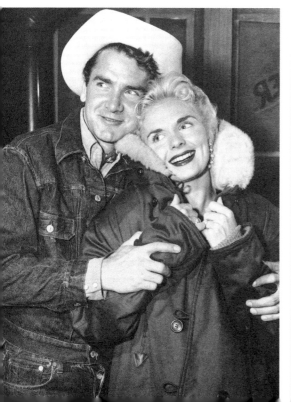 

have enough ambition. For the first time in my life, I settled for just continuing on what was certainly a dead-end path.

Despondent though I was over Mary's death, I was raised as a Roman Catholic by strict parents, so it was ingrained in me to believe in the power of prayer and God's plan for all of us. Even at that terrible moment when I found out my baby was dead, I know that the first thing I did was close my eyes and whisper, "Thy will be done."

So I never stopped praying. Every morning before going to work, I attended Mass at St. Mary's of the Point in downtown Pittsburgh, just a few blocks from the KDKA studios. I truly believed that one day God would answer my prayers and allow me to bring a healthy baby into the world.

The summer of '57 dragged on, me in a fog, work in a rut, when out of nowhere I got a surprising phone call from a man named Fred Burleigh, who was the director of the Pittsburgh Playhouse. The Pittsburgh Playhouse was considered "big theatre" in our town, with two stages, one on Craft Avenue and the other on Hazlett Street. Only very experienced actors performed there, and it was rumored around town that Burleigh was looking for a blockbuster to help celebrate the Playhouse's 25th anniversary season.

The play he chose was *Bus Stop*, a proven Broadway hit that became even bigger when it was turned into a movie starring Marilyn Monroe. *Bus Stop* may have been perfect for the Pittsburgh Playhouse, but Burleigh was having trouble casting the perfect female lead.

So it was quite a shock to find Fred Burleigh himself on the other end of my telephone, inviting me to audition. The only acting I had ever done was summer stock at the Little Lake Theatre, and that was just a lark, something fun to take up the time. But this was *huge*. I'd heard the buzz around town that a big-time actor was being brought in from New York to the play the leading male role.

I was in no mood to do anything other than trudge to work and drag myself home again at the end of the day, but I suppose it's one of life's little tricks to push you back among the world of the living after you experience tragedy. Figuring I had nothing to lose, I set out for the audition. Now, if you're not familiar with *Bus Stop*, let me tell you that it's the story of a small town girl who gets stranded for three days at a Kansas bus stop during a raging snow storm. The play is a one-set production, with two bit-players — a sheriff and a waitress — plus the leads, Bo the cowboy, and Cheri, the chanteuse (which she pronounces "chan-too-sey").

Entering that theatre for my audition, I can tell you I honestly hadn't been so nervous since the day I marched into Jay Reich's advertising agency and told him I could do a better job than the man narrating my fashion commercials. That bout of nerves only increased when I was introduced to Gaines Kincaid, the professional actor who would play the part of Bo. He was *gorgeous!*

We were given a few lines and about two minutes to rehearse. That wasn't a problem for me; I was used to memorizing scripts for TV commercials. But then I heard a voice booming through the darkness and I started to shake all over again.

"Ms. Schano, I would like you to get up on that round table and sing 'That Old Black Magic.' And lift your skirt so I can see your legs."

"Uhhh. . . Mr. Burleigh . . . I can't sing," I mumbled into the darkened theatre. By that point, I was hoping he'd just tell me to get off the stage and go home, but instead, he took me aside and explained that the character Cheri was a "chan-too-sey" who only *thought* she could sing.

"Marilyn Monroe couldn't sing either," Burleigh added.

And so I climbed up on that table, showed him my legs, and belted out the worst rendition of 'That Old Black Magic' you ever heard. On September 5, 1957, *Bus Stop* opened at the Pittsburgh

Playhouse's Craft Avenue Theatre, and the marquee out front announced its stars: Gaines Kincaid and Eleanor Schano. *Bus Stop* played for the next sixteen weeks to standing-room only audiences.

At about the same time *Bus Stop* opened at the Playhouse, my life took a miraculous turn. God answered my prayers and I became pregnant with my second child. The news brought me out of my fog, and with it, the energy to go back to work at KDKA with some enthusiasm.

By that time, my husband's life had taken some turns, too. Warren left his job at KDKA and tried several other positions elsewhere but ultimately he just didn't want to pursue a career in television. He was a cerebral person with varied interests and broadcasting never did stir in him any great feelings of satisfaction or excitement.

Warren and I decided that I would continue to work as long as I could hide my pregnancy (once again, loose-fitting fashions worked in my favor), making me the family's main breadwinner. I didn't mind. After all, my energy and enthusiasm for life, career included, had returned once I found out I was pregnant again. So to work every day I went.

As my due-date approached, I ricocheted between apprehension and trust that everything would be okay. On a gentle spring morning in April, 1958, it was time to set out for the hospital, and despite what had happened the last time, I was returning to the same hospital where Mary had been born and then so tragically died. Women *do* fall in love with their obstetricians and since that's where *he* was that's where I would go to deliver this second baby.

I found myself back in that same awful labor room but this time only one other bed was occupied. My labor was easier than the first one too, and within hours I knew the indescribable joy of cradling my perfectly healthy, perfectly beautiful infant daughter, Jennifer.

Life for me was now complete. I felt back on track, and returned to work at KDKA reinvigorated, often bringing Jennifer with me whenever I could. For the first time in a long time, I was hopeful not just for the future of my family, but also for the future of my career. By the autumn of 1958, Pittsburgh's third television station went on the air. WTAE-TV began broadcasting and I finally decided it was time to join the exodus of colleagues leaving KDKA and search for new opportunities at WTAE.

In sharp contrast to KDKA's downtown studios, WTAE built their facility about five miles east of the city between Wilkinsburg and Monroeville. WIIC TV had already been on the air for a year, but it wasn't until WTAE TV arrived on the scene that the competition really got serious. KDKA had lost its monopoly on local news, and stations had figured out that the newscasts could generate a primary source of revenue.

WTAE lured TV veteran — and my pal — Dave Murray as its news director, and he brought with him news editor George Thomas, plus several crack TV news photographers like Fred DiFiore and Charlie McGrath. Since I'd known Dave Murray dating back to our days at WDTV, I thought I might finally have the edge I needed to move into TV news. I quickly discovered it wasn't going to be that easy.

The 15-minute format for the early evening news was new, with sports and a brief weather forecast rounding out the program. But then, the sales department realized it could sell advertising for *each* of those segments and basically triple its commercial dollars for one newscast. So with the weather now a separate element and sponsored by a different client it no longer made sense to have the newsman just rattle off a brief forecast.

Word soon spread among the broadcasting community that WTAE would sign the Bell Telephone Company as the sponsor for its weather. With all of my earlier experience as The Weather Girl at WDTV, I figured I might as well get on the phone and try to convince Dave Murray to give me a shot at the job. Once again, I realized as I dialed the phone, I was trying to find a "back door" into a newsroom, but they all seemed to have the same symbolic sign on the door: No Women Need Apply.

Dave explained the decision about the weather segment wasn't up to him, that it would be made by the big Philadelphia advertising agency Gray and Rogers, who sent their rep Chet Cooper to Pittsburgh to hold open auditions for the spokesman spot.

And I do place the emphasis on spokes*man*.

Dave Murray knew the news business like no one else and that also extended to knowing how to say "no." He may have been my friend, but he made it crystal clear that as a woman, I wouldn't be welcome at that audition. I pleaded, then begged, until he finally shot back, "Eleanor, the agency wants a man for this role. I have 28 men already lined up for the audition so there is no need for us to have any more conversation about it." And then he hung up.

However, I felt there *was* a need for us to have more conversation about it, and for the next two days I placed a couple of dozen phone calls to Dave until he finally broke down and took my call. After his terse *hello*, I didn't even give him the chance to speak.

"Dave, I know what you said, but I'm willing to take any chance at all that the client might take a look at me. *Please* let me come."

I could hear his sigh over the phone line. At that point, he just wanted me to go away, so he said, "Okay, Eleanor, you can come. . . but you have to understand that you *will not get hired.*"

"Yeah, sure, I understand," I assured him. "If nothing else it will give me a chance to see the new TV station."

And so it was, with outward bravado and inward dread, I set out for the WTAE studios the following Monday morning. The room I was escorted into was literally overflowing with men, some short, some tall, all ages, all sizes. Some I recognized and others I'd never even seen around town. Apparently it was preferable to audition a guy who had probably never even seen a television studio to a woman who had already been working at one for almost a decade!

We all waited. The men engaged in nervous small talk. I just sat there, largely ignored. Finally, Dave Murray walked in and introduced everyone to the ad agency's rep, Chet Cooper. Cooper's eyes moved quickly over the group in the room, kind of like a little league coach hoping to spot a potential star player among the ragtag kids who show up just hoping to make the team.

Chet Cooper's gaze did not so much as even pause on me. I was invisible, not even a contender. That much was clear.

Within minutes, he called the men in alphabetical order and asked them to line up outside the studio. I was furious. Not surprised, mind you, but furious. I found a chair near the studio door and sat down for what turned out to be the next two hours, watching and waiting as each man took his turn going into the studio to audition. When the last man came out, I made my move. I literally knocked past this man and strode right onto the studio floor. It happened so fast that the cameras and their operators were still in place.

"Hello, everyone! Let me introduce myself!" I called brightly to the room at large. "My name is Eleanor Schano and I am a woman just asking for a minute of your time." Dave Murray was in the control room with Chet Cooper so I couldn't see him from where I was, but I was sure he probably turned beet red and was ready to explode at my audacity. But I'd come too far to back down, so I just kept on talking. "I apologize for auditioning like this, but I have experience and I would like you to consider me for the position of spokesperson."

The cameramen were slack-jawed and shocked, and I think I probably looked the same way a moment later when a message came from the control room to the studio. It was a deep male voice definitely tinged with impatience.

"Let her read the prompter but tell her to make it quick."

It was my big chance — and I met it with a big problem. I had terrible eyesight and couldn't see a word of the commercial script typed on the TV Teleprompter! I felt like Cheri back on the set of *Bus Stop* — only this time instead of being the "chan-too-sey" who couldn't sing, I was the broadcaster who couldn't read!

"Once again, I have to apologize," I called back sweetly, my bright smile never faltering. "Bad eyesight; can't see the promptor. I'll just have to ad-lib."

I launched into a rapid-fire schpeil and it was an argument meant to persuade. I was in front of a camera, a place that was familiar, a place where I felt more comfortable than just about any other spot on the planet. And with hands on my hips, I told them exactly why they'd be wise to hire a woman for this job instead of a man.

"As a woman, I know and care more about your product than any man. After all, what woman doesn't love a telephone! Also, we make most of the decisions about how many telephones we'll have in the home, we pick the color and the style. Why, I just love your new Princess model! I ordered two for my house last week!"

I babbled on and on about the great service my local Bell Telephone Company provided until someone finally jumped in and told me to wrap it up.

Another big smile, a "Thank you so much for your kind attention," and then I grabbed my things and made a hasty exit before Dave Murray could find me and wring my neck.

On the drive home, I had the good grace to feel embarrassed. It's one thing to be assertive, but another thing entirely to knock down a door and push your way inside. My Grandma Daley's words came to the rescue. She would say, "No need to cry over spilled milk."

So, as soon as I walked in the front door of my home, I picked up Jennifer from her crib and left the incident at the WTAE

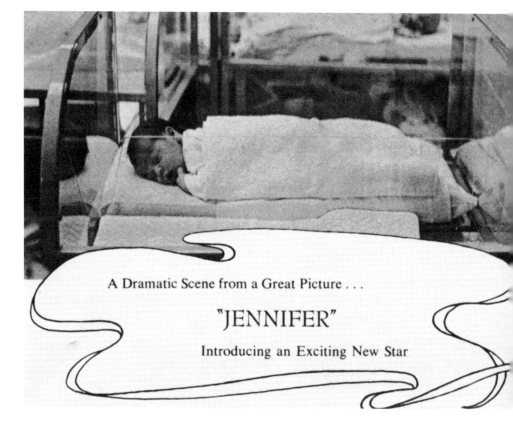

A Dramatic Scene from a Great Picture . . .

"JENNIFER"

Introducing an Exciting New Star

▲ April 28th, 1958

◀ Eleanor at 8½ months pregnant, April 14, 1958. Disguising my pregnancy at a time when you couldn't even mention the word on television. The fashions of the day helped to camouflage my condition and allowed me to keep me job.

studio behind me. The next morning the weather was bright and clear — a rarity for a November day in Pittsburgh — so I bundled up my daughter and we took a nice long stroll in the park. I didn't think about the previous day's disastrous audition because when you aren't even in the running for the job, it's easy to put it out of your mind. I had just put Jennifer down for her nap when the telephone rang — one of my new Bell Telephone Princess model phones, to be exact. It was a familiar voice at the other end.

"Uhh, Eleanor, it's Dave Murray."

Here it comes, I thought. The reaming out he didn't get to give me the day before.

Instead, he said, "I'm not sure that I know exactly what's going on but Chet Cooper would like to meet with you tomorrow morning. Can you be here at 10:30?" In total disbelief, I told him sure, but before he hung up, he added in a very gentle tone, "Don't get your hopes up. The Bell Telephone Company has never used a female spokesperson before. I really have no idea why Chet wants to see you."

I arrived early for that appointment the next morning and while I waited, my mind raced with the possibilities, which ranged from wondering if I was going to get a big lecture about professional behavior to worrying that this was going to be a repeat of some of those lecherous scenes from my earlier days in the business.

What I *wasn't* prepared for was for the door to swing open to reveal that same man whose eyes had passed over me completely at the audition the day before now resting so warmly and directly on me, with outstretched arms and a smile on his face.

"Ms. Schano, I hope I haven't kept you waiting!" he exclaimed, then led me solicitously into the office. As we walked there, as he pulled out a chair for me to sit, Chet Cooper explained that he had the difficult task of talking with each of the men who had auditioned, telling them that they had not been selected for the position.

I kept my smile in place but my brain was buzzing! Was that why *I* was here, to be told I hadn't gotten the position, either? Or was he saying that *they* hadn't gotten the position because it was going to me? And then he broke into an amiable grin.

"I must say, I was impressed with your performance yesterday. You're a spunky young lady and my client has agreed to take a chance on you."

A spunky young lady...

Okay, I could live with that, so long as it got me the job. But I didn't have too long to bask in the joy because he continued to explain, in a more serious tone, "As you know, we've never hired a woman before and we're making a big exception for you. I trust it will not be a mistake. There are those who believe women are just not as... *dependable*... as men."

Wow. I heard that message loud and clear: *Make sure you don't go and do something as undependable as get pregnant!*

And so it was that I went on the air as the weathercaster for WTAE TV, sponsored by the esteemed Bell Telephone Company, on December 15, 1958.

My second daughter Lorie was born on November 21, 1959. You do the math!

****

Since I had no desire to confirm my new sponsor's opinion that women were not as dependable as men, I decided to keep my little secret about expecting my second child. That doesn't mean I wasn't thrilled by the news. I was bursting inside and it was a chore not to share that excitement with everyone I passed on the street *but* I also liked my new career move to WTAE TV and I didn't want to see the job go to someone else on a technicality.

As the months wore on, I wondered how long I could hide my condition, but the boxy Chanel jacket was *in* and I found that it camouflaged my expanding figure. This worked *so well* that I was able to go on the air right up until the night before I delivered my baby! When my studio crew learned the next day that I was in the hospital they sent a bouquet of flowers with a "Get Well" card attached.

It might be commonplace today for a new parent to take up to twelve weeks of maternity leave, but such luxuries didn't exist in 1959, so I simply put in for my two weeks' vacation time to get Lorie home and settled, and then I was back to work. The guys at WTAE were some of my best friends — they couldn't believe I hadn't let them in on my secret that I had been pregnant all those months! — and they greeted me with a portable changing station and several months' supply of diapers. They were used to seeing me bring my first daughter, Jennifer, to work with me from time to time. She was 18 months old when Lorie was born, and the crew guys told me they hoped I'd bring *both* girls to the station now!

I had in place a very good support system at home. I had hired a wonderful babysitter, a woman named Alice who had already raised a family and treated my children like her own. Don't get the wrong idea, I can't say going back to work and leaving a two-week-old and an 18-month-old at home even for a brief period of time was easy, but I felt reassured by the knowledge that she was providing them with loving care during my absence from home — which was rarely more than 3 hours at a time. Since I was assigned to appear on both the Noon and 6 p.m. news my schedule at WTAE-TV was split and I came home for several hours between shows. And when Alice couldn't make it, I simply took the girls to work with me. On more than one occasion, the crew guys made good on their promise and took turns babysitting while I was on the air!

I felt as if my life were on track again, the "happily ever after" young girls dream of. I felt challenged and satisfied by work, and I was ecstatic to have my two daughters— turning into adorable little toddlers right in front of my eyes — but I also remember feeling terminally exhausted! Three babies in four years and a demanding job saps a lot of energy even when you're young.

Life was a whirlwind of changing hats from my TV persona to wife, mom, cook, chauffeur, laundress, cleaning woman. I would bolt into the house after work . . . kick off my high heels . . . tie on the apron . . . cook dinner, feed husband, bathe children, read bedtime stories, listen to the girls' nightly prayers, then do the laundry and top off the night by boning up on the next day's assignments back at the TV station. The days flew by in a blur.

Warren was home quite a lot since he was again between jobs, preferring to pursue hobbies — photography and model railroading were particular favorites— while waiting for a more satisfying job opportunity to come his way. I felt the pressure of being the sole wage earner in the family during very lean years, but I never brought those frustrations out into the open. He viewed what I did as just another job. Remember, he grew up surrounded by movie stars, since his dad had been a top exec at Universal Pictures. When Daddy regularly brings Judy Garland home for dinner, how impressed can you be by your wife's job doing commercials at the local television station? It paid the bills and that was what mattered.

I chalked it all up to the usual tribulations of marriage and simply forged ahead. He had flaws, but what human doesn't? He was a fine man with many good qualities, he loved our daughters, and everything we did, we did for them or with them. (I particularly recall one Christmas, when Warren and I spent every night for three weeks making a big gingerbread house from scratch.) I assessed my many roles and realized I may have been

Eleanor Schano at work, but at home I was Warren's wife and Jennifer and Lorie's mom. Considering all I'd been through in the past decade, the *status quo* seemed fine. More than fine. It was hectic but challenging, and if not perfect, at least it felt safe.

I could not begin to guess how much that would change in the not-too-distant future.

●

Mother's Day 1960

4

Battling the Mommy Wars

It was the dawn of a new decade — the early 1960's — and around the newsroom talk was of racial tensions in cities across America . . . Alaska becoming the 49th US state . . . the significance of Martin Luther King's "I have a dream" speech. . . . and Fidel Castro's successful revolution against Cuban dictator Fulgencio Batista.

Here at home, thousands of Pittsburghers showed up to hear Soviet Premier Nikita Kruschev speak for peace . . . Senator John F. Kennedy and Richard Nixon made Pittsburgh a stop on the campaign trail, visiting the city within twelve days of each other . . . and Bill Mazeroski hit a ninth-inning homerun in game seven of the World Series so the Pirates could defeat the New York Yankees, giving Pittsburgh its first World Series championship in 35 years.

Witnessing those events — and watching the newsroom reporters cover them — only added more fuel to the fire burning within me to join their ranks. For awhile there, during the mid-

1950's just after the death of my first daughter, I had lost my will, lost my way, but my energy had returned and my goals were back on track now. I watched the activity buzzing in the newsroom like the kid pressing her nose against the candy store window. I wanted to be one of *them*. Instead, I was doing the weather, and even though I was happier in my new work environment than I had been in my last days at KDKA, doing the weather night after night became more than a little dull.

Despite that, I had a great record of never taking a day off work — and anyone with little kids knows what a feat that is! Today you might find progressive companies offering on-site daycare, and in a way I'm sure WTAE never intended, they offered it to me, too. Paul Shannon did an afternoon program called *Adventure Time* featuring some *Three Stooges* episodes interspersed with silly antics on set. The show had a live audience of kids and any time my baby-sitter Alice was unable to show up, I simply brought Jennifer and Lorie to the studio and let them sit in the *Adventure Time* audience. I had peace of mind, and no one ever suspected that I had to bring the girls with me because of child care issues. Plus, my daughters loved it!

There were dozens of other perks. Our art director Joe Bach took the girls' orders every year and made their Halloween costumes, which were incredible. One year Jennifer was a witch and the hat Joe made was so sturdy that it lasted long enough for Jennifer's daughters to wear decades later! Lorie was an angel with the biggest wings you can imagine . . . all sparkling with diamond dust and gold lamé. They both won the contest at the Fire Hall that season.

For awhile they thought being hauled back and forth to the studio was just a normal part of growing up, that everyone's Mom was on TV. I also brought them along any time I had a personal appearance, such as parades, fairs, and community gatherings. They were used to the public recognition I received in supermarkets and restaurants. Sometimes people would whisper as we passed them on the street, "Isn't that Eleanor

Schano?" and one time my daughter piped up, "No, she's my mom."

I felt like I had assumed a double identity: When I was ON I was Eleanor Schano, Local TV Celebrity; and when I was OFF I was the wife and mom who took care of the kids, who went to the bank and dry-cleaners, picked up milk at the corner market, and took the trash to the curb on Wednesday nights.

While doing the weather was dull, being the spokesperson for the Bell Telephone Company offered incredible opportunities to do and see things that I never would have had in any other situation. Even though none of us were meteorologists (few weathercasters were in the '60's) — and I was the only woman among them — the company believed that weather reporters should have a thorough knowledge of the science. Education seminars were held each year and the most memorable for me was attending a briefing at the National Hurricane Center in Miami before being taken up with a hurricane hunter during an actual storm.

Yes, I did it. Flew into the eye of a hurricane. It was a spectacular adventure.

"Fasten your safety belt, we're going in," the pilot shouted over the roar of the turbulence. Was I frightened? There are no words to describe the terror I felt — heart pounding, a golf-ball-sized lump in my throat making it impossible to swallow. But the moment we entered the eye of the storm, I thought that it must be a lot like what astronauts feel when they fly into space because for those few moments I was suspended in a time warp where everything stood still — an eerie calm I had never experienced before.

Other seminars took us to Kennedy Space Center in Florida where we were granted special VIP treatment, meeting with NASA officials and going up into the huge vehicle assembly building; and to the Massachusetts Institute of Technology (MIT) oceanographic center, where our group met with the scientists who study weather patterns and their effects on the planet.

These trips were infrequent and usually lasted just three or four days, and while I hated to leave my kids I knew they were well taken care of. Warren was there, my mom lived close by, and we had an excellent babysitter. The girls usually were so indulged during my absence that they looked at these infrequent trips of mine as mini-holidays!

Back then I was the oddball working mom in the neighborhood, so sure, there were times I felt pangs of guilt. Today, the working mom scenario is a common one, but the guilt issue is still the same. Magazines devote whole sagas to the issue of "Mommy Wars," i.e. should moms work outside the home or not? Women supposedly line up on either side of the debate and the tactic, they say, is to defend your choice by criticizing the other side's choice.

You didn't find scientific studies chronicling the effects — or lack thereof — of working moms in the early 1960's, but I can tell you from reporting and researching all these years that for any scientific study that "proves" one thing, there most certainly is another scientific study "proving" exactly the opposite. All I can do is speak from my own personal experience, and what I learned is, children are resilient.

Quality still outweighs quantity when it comes to child-rearing, so do your best when you're with them and that will stretch over into the gaps when you aren't there. I've interviewed hundreds of women on this topic and came across many stay-at-home moms who face their own challenges, managing the stresses and details of day-to-day life with little kids, and *they* often long for some stimuli *outside* the home to recharge their batteries.

I've come to believe it's a matter of balance, and think *all* women, whether they work inside *or* outside of the home, need to find time to nurture their own dreams as attentively as they nurture their children. I don't think my own daughters suffered from my absence when I was at work, but I firmly believe they would have been horribly shortchanged if I was *mentally absent* during the times I was at home with them.

Of course, this "wise old advice" comes after *five decades of learning the hard way*, but even back in the early days of the 1960's, I felt there was some message to share, something about the changing role of women in our society and I took this hazy idea to work. The News Director was Fred Remington, a man whose former job had been Radio/TV editor over at the *Pittsburgh Press*. Not exactly a background for running a TV news department! I trudged into his office often, always begging for a chance to prove that I could handle hard news. Fred never bit, no matter how I cast the line.

I tweaked my pitch and eventually proposed a documentary on the changing roles of women. Fred finally agreed to give me a shot at it, *except* he added, "You can do it on your own time," which meant *no pay*.

No pay and extra work. Wow. What an honor, I thought derisively.

But I *did* do it. A crummy chance was better than *no chance*, after all.

It was called *The Vanishing Female* — not a title I like, in retrospect — but the point I wanted to get across at the time was that female roles that had been defined *before* World War II were vanishing, and a *new* species had surfaced. Rosie the Riveter led the march for women to assume new roles in government, business, science, labor, and entertainment.

My research focused on the number of women entering the workforce. I offered not only statistics but job opportunities as well, and I interviewed Ann X. Alpern, the first woman to sit on the Pennsylvania Supreme Court; a local woman named Arlene Miller, whose love of the arts and painting led to her opening an art gallery in Kaufmann's Department Store; and Theresa Rocco, the Pittsburgh Police Captain who headed up the Missing Persons Division.

Writing, producing and narrating that project was exhilarating! I stretched my wings beyond reporting the weather, turning those Brenda Starr fantasies of my youth into the real, live thing. I loved asking the tough questions, I loved the fact that what I produced could be a contribution to the fledging dialogue about women's rights and equality, could even make a huge difference in the quality of a viewer's life!

Well, *The Vanishing Female* certainly made a difference in *my* life, because it won the prestigious Golden Quill Award, and earned me new respect from my male colleagues in the newsroom.

In fact, one of the highest compliments came from a colleague with tons of talent, loads of confidence, and a booming voice that sounded like God Himself was speaking. His name: Paul Long.

Paul said, "You've got it, kid. I'll bet my money on your future in this news business."

I was flying high off such high praise coming from a man so respected as a reporter.

That's a funny thing, actually. Paul Long and so many of the others went on to earn the highest honors and accolades in the broadcasting business, and viewers only have the image of them as venerable and *serious* TV reporters. *I* got to see the *other* side of those guys, and let me tell you, one of the best fringe benefits of working at WTAE was that cast of characters who filled the newsroom. It could have been a sit-com!

My desk was next to Paul Long. He wrote all of his own scripts and if I learned anything from him it was about integrity, ethics, getting it right, and keeping it short. I greatly admired his work, and he became a dear friend. He took my dreams to work on the news side of the business seriously and took me under his wing, showing me all there was to know about writing a tight news story with a compelling sense of urgency.

We remained lifelong friends and I even delivered one of the eulogies at his funeral several years back, and it is *because* we were such dear friends that I am able to say, in all honesty, that Paul Long was a curmudgeon. Correction: A *lovable* curmudgeon.

Paul was not one for caring much about how he looked. He only had two suits—one brown and one blue, and he wore the same pair of penny loafers the entire time I knew him. I kept three ties in my desk drawer for those times when he would come back from lunch with either tomato soup (his favorite) or mustard splattered over the entire front of his neckpiece. It didn't bother him but I insisted that viewers might be a tiny bit distracted by the stains instead of listening to the news he was reporting.

My favorite Paul Long anecdote: Once, when he was coming back from a field assignment with another reporter, they decided to drive through a fast-food joint to order lunch. After the cameraman and the other reporter gave their orders, Paul's voice boomed from the backseat, "I'll have a cheeseburger and a double Rob Roy." The worker at the other end of the drive-through speaker stammered, "We don't have Rob Roys," and just as fast Paul shot back, "Then I'll have a beer."

And I'll always remember the day a bouncy, verbose, boyishly handsome man strode into the newsroom and General Manager John Conomikes announced, "I want you to meet the very best news anchor in the United States. I found him in Chicago. Meet Don Cannon."

Don Cannon and Paul Long went on to co-host WTAE's news for a 25-year stretch, and I loved to watch the way they interacted, how they discussed and debated the content of their news scripts.

Although my husband Warren was no longer in the business, most of our friends were and since money was tight and babysitters were scarce for everyone, we all entertained ourselves by hosting little dinner parties for each other. Frequent dinner guests in my home included Bill and Jean Burns, who lived just a few miles away. Later Dan Mallinger (my old friend from my early career days at *Packaged Programs*) and his wife Marlene became nearby neighborhoods, as well. Al and Mame McDowell and Bob and Pat Dickey . . . we were all together, young, so serious about our careers, yet so good-natured about our friendships and sharing and supporting each other.

I almost think of that crowd as separate characters from the people we've all grown to be — some still in the business, some retired, some gone too soon from this world. I can't help but smile and shake my head and think we were young and idealistic and driven by dreams — but good at heart and always inspired by a genuine desire to serve the audience by reporting the news and reporting it well.

I know that remained *my* genuine desire. I was flying high off the experience of producing that documentary about women's changing roles, and thrilled at its success, but unfortunately it still wasn't enough to convince News-Director-Fred that I was ready to handle the heavy-lifting of hard news. But it *was* enough to get him to start giving me some "soft" feature assignments. And to be honest, instead of being grateful, I kind of hated it. When you're watching your colleagues race out of the newsroom to cover a fire or crime, it's not much of a consolation prize to know that you are covering the annual flower show or attending a tea in honor of the Governor's wife.

Yawn. . .

But I did it, just as I continued doing the weather — and then another most unexpected opportunity came my way and it led to another broadcast "first" — a television series in national syndication!

It all began innocently enough. One summer evening I took my girls on an errand to Grace's Store on Bower Hill Road in Scott Township. I needed milk and the girls — aged 4 and 2½ at the time — were angling for boxes of animal crackers. We rounded the corner of an aisle and happened to bump into my friend Dan Mallinger.

We chatted for a few minutes and then Dan casually asked, "What would you think about doing a syndicated television series?"

I have to tell you a little bit about Grace's Store so you can truly appreciate the scene. If you couldn't find what you needed at Grace's you probably didn't need it. It was a general store where you went to buy anything from groceries to hardware to auto supplies and lumber. Friends and neighbors would meet and discuss their golf scores, their kids' bout with measles, or in the case of Eleanor Schano and Dan Mallinger, an idea for a syndicated TV series.

My daughters were getting impatient but the promise of those animal crackers quieted them down for a little while longer as Dan told me about his friend Ken Israel, and a little idea the two of them had been kicking around. Ken was convinced the national market was ripe for another series of 15-minute programs, and since he was a topnotch salesman, he had no doubt that he could sell the right product into national syndication. The trick, of course, was finding the right product.

It was a heady notion, for sure! No one had ever dreamed of taking a local program into national syndication. Most programming came out of Hollywood or New York, usually low-budget black and white stuff with a star of some name value.

I told him it sounded like a fantastic opportunity, but privately, I chalked it all up to a nice pipe dream, bid him goodbye, and dragged my girls off in search of those animal crackers. So you can imagine my surprise when my phone rang the next day and Dan was at the other end of it, asking if I could

New .... Fresh ...
Completely different!

* 130 fifteen minute episodes
  or
* 195 ten minute episodes
  or
* 390 five minute episodes
* Produced on film specifically for TV.
* Primarily dealing with Face ... Figure ... and Fashion.
* Hundreds of thought-provoking tips on Charm, Beauty, Good Grooming.
* Of interest to women of all ages ... including teen-agers.
* A sure loyal audience builder.
* Includes every dimension of self-improvement.

Gateway to Glamour

Eleanor Schano

Excellent sales vehicle for television! Powerful commercial value!

* An excitement of ideas, well communicated and dramatically presented.
* An additional special feature in each show "Figure control tip for Today".
* "GlamoRecord" available at no additional cost for reproduction and distribution by station or sponsor.
* Eleanor is available for personal appearances and commercials.

Gateway to Glamour WITH *Eleanor Schano*
BUILDS AUDIENCES! CREATES SALES!

VARIETY
Film Pastures Reap Harvest

▼ *Dan Mallinger, Eleanor, Fred DiFiore*

meet with him and Ken Israel to brainstorm about the pilot episode of this supposed nationally syndicated series.

I liked and trusted Dan, and I'd been acquainted with Ken Israel — the production community was small, after all, and we tended to know who was who — so I agreed to the meeting. Twenty-four hours later, the three of us were seated in Dan's living room, drawing on the creative juices and dreaming big.

A very popular daytime series at that time starred psychologist Dr. Joyce Brothers of *The $64,000 Quiz Show* fame, and another starred fitness guru Jack LaLanne. Dan and Ken felt certain that if they had the right kind of product to appeal to the same audience that watched those shows, we could really strike it big.

Knowing the program had to appeal to women, we started kicking around possibilities based on some of my personal experiences. For several years during my college days, I taught "charm" classes to high school students at Kaufmanns, and self-improvement and grooming classes to young women attending a local business school. Ideas started to gel and we came up with a program we titled *Gateway to Glamour*. Dan Mallinger would produce it, Ken Israel would sell it — and I would write it and be the on-camera host. I immediately got to work on an outline for the pilot.

To syndicate, we would need a whole lot of product, 390 five-minutes segments total! Stations could either air them as five *or* ten-minute drop-ins during a local show or they could string three together for a fifteen minute stand-alone program. Dan Mallinger returned to Packaged Programs once more to hire a photographer — my old pal Fred DiFiore — and editor Jay Gould. We rented space and designed a set.

Maybe "designed" is a little too grandiose to describe what we did. This set consisted of a borrowed table from Gimbel's Department Store, a lattice-backed chair, and a drape to cover the bare studio wall. We're not talking "low budget," we're talking "*no* budget!"

I stood among those humble props and beamed a smile and ad-libbed my way through the finer points of fashion, face and figure.

Voila! Gateway to Glamour!

With one program in the can, Ken Israel took off to test waters and see if he could find any interest in *Gateway to Glamour* starring Eleanor Schano — not a name known outside of Western Pennsylvania. Ken's first stop was WWJ in Detroit, Michigan, and his instincts proved correct because it just so happened the program manager at WWJ had been scouting around for a program to air adjacent to Jack LaLanne. He looked at our pilot, liked it, and bought the entire series on the spot for $35,000.

The only problem was, *there was no series.* We only had one episode!

Ken didn't bother to mention that teensy, insignificant detail to the program manager, just came on back and calmly informed Dan and me that we had a deal, and we had to start delivering episodes in *three weeks!*

Our eyeballs must have bugged out of our heads but Ken pointed out that WWJ had signed a contract and paid the money up front. Plus, WWJ had immediately gone to work on publicity, so by the time Ken was back home informing us of this spectacular — and terrifying — development, promos were already running in Detroit for *Stay Fit with Jack LaLanne* followed by *Gateway to Glamour with Eleanor Schano.*

All we could do was dive in and get to work on the shows.

With no time to write full scripts, I delivered outlines of each program to Dan, and then ad-libbed once the cameras were rolling. Thank heavens for all those years of modeling experience, plus the grooming classes I had taught, even all those weekend mornings I'd put in on the teen fashion board! I had no lack of material to fill the shows, and it was an exhilarating challenge to get through the whirlwind tape schedule.

Considering today's television shows featuring extreme makeovers, what we covered on *Gateway to Glamour* would be considered mighty tame. Imagine segments on how to apply leg make-up to cover varicose veins . . . clothing to camouflage figure flaws . . . little hair and make-ups tips. But back then, it was hot hot hot advice, and I burned through it, even going so far as starting off the segment with no make-up and demo'ing the technique on myself! You might call it the precursor to reality TV — or you might just say we didn't have the budget for a model!

Meanwhile, Ken put together a snappy little brochure in addition to our pilot, and armed with that sales kit, he continued to travel around the country wrapping up deals. We were in dozens of markets before we even finished production.

For the next five months, we shot five fifteen-minute shows every Monday, Wednesday and Friday. Jay would edit them on Tuesday and Thursday, then ship them out to Detroit. More like *Gateway to a Nervous Breakdown!* The story of this grueling production schedule even made news in the trade publications. To this day, no one can believe we filmed and edited and delivered 390 TV programs in just five months, with the show ultimately running in several hundred markets around the country.

A funny sidebar: One station that *didn't* carry *Gateway to Glamour* was WTAE TV, where I was still appearing daily as the weathercaster and features reporter! Ken Israel assumed that WTAE naturally would buy the series since I was on-air there, but when they didn't jump at his offer, he went across town and offered it to WIIC TV. They *did* jump, earning me another broadcast "first," although this one a little more dubious than my other distinctions. I was the first performer ever to appear on competing television stations in the same market at the same time. Mornings on WIIC and evenings on WTAE.

I look back on the whole swift, sweet experience with just one regret: I have only a couple of the original *Gateway to*

Glamour programs. Once the series had run its course, Ken Israel sold them for the value of the celluloid. So much of early television was never archived.

But I will never forget that crazy five-month period and anytime since when people say, "Wow, television must be so glamorous," I can't help but smile and think of *Gateway to Glamour*. In just five months, we cranked out 390 programs on a production budget of $35,000!

Everyone thinks television is so glamorous, but let me tell you, the only "glamour" is in the finished product, friends. What happens behind the scenes is a whole other story!

***

Getting on the air and *staying* on the air were not necessarily the same thing. One might get a job in TV but to keep it, you had to "research well." TV stations hired research firms to conduct surveys among viewers and if you "researched well" you were in. If they determined that you "did *not* research well," you'd better polish up the resume because you'd be out, *fast!*

Being on WTAE as the weathergirl and as a feature reporter *plus* being seen in *Gateway to Glamour* on WIIC-TV at the same time gave me great exposure, and as a result I "researched well."

Yet I still recall the General Manager, Franklin Snyder, saying to me one day, "I have no idea why you are more recognizable than some of our newsmen."

I wanted to shake the guy! If I was so much more recognizable, I wondered, why not let me tackle the tough stuff and make the popular TV persona pay off!? But even though it seemed like I was caught in the quicksand of "soft news," I truly believed all of my waiting and watching and learning and hoping were about to pay off. Don't ask me how, I just *felt* it.

And surely enough, my chance finally came.

A news story broke that left the city in shock. A young woman was gang-raped. The suspects — a group of motorcycle toughs — had been arrested and were to be arraigned at the Wilkinsburg Police Station located less than five minutes from the WTAE studios. I noticed in some news footage that had been taken early in the morning that the victim was there as well, being escorted into the police station along with the seven men accused.

Now, sexual assault was a subject swept under the rug in those days. We didn't talk about such things in public, let alone on television. The crime itself was distasteful enough and left the city's collective jaw dropping, and no news station intended to get into the details of the rape itself.

Every other WTAE crew was out on assignment but when one news photographer returned from a fire — his hair still smelled from the smoke — I grabbed his arm and literally dragged him back toward the door, calling casually to the news director, "Hey, Fred, we're going to cover that arraignment down the street."

I didn't *ask* if we could go, I just announced it and then beat it fast. If Fred was gong to tell me "no," he'd have to do it by two-way radio because I was gone before he ever had the chance to respond.

By the time we arrived at the police station, crews from all the local radio and TV stations were swarming the building. Everyone rushed in to get footage of the seven suspects, but I took a detour to ask an officer where the *victim* was. He pointed in the direction of the ladies room down the hall and so, with adrenaline surging through every vein in my body I set off in that direction.

The door opened with a squeak, and across the room stood a ghostly pale young woman, trembling in her effort to hold back tears. At that moment, I was overcome with anger at the way crime can reduce a person, how it took a pretty young woman and left her bruised, terrified, and shaking with tears in a dirty police station bathroom. I don't know if I was a news reporter or just another woman aching with sympathy at that moment, but our eyes met and then I was next to her and it just seemed natural to open my arms and pull her in. She collapsed against me and we stood like that for several minutes, letting the silence calm our nerves.

When she lifted her head at last, her eyes were clear and they met mine head on.

"I know who you are. I see you on television."

She started to stumble through the details of the rape, unconsciously clutching my hand, and it was clear to me that she was anxious to talk, anxious to have someone listen. I was extremely moved that she trusted *me* to be that person.

"Do you want to tell your story on TV?" I finally asked her, and when I saw the hesitation flicker in her eyes I quickly added, "We'll protect your identity." That did it. She firmly nodded *yes*. "Wait here," I told her, giving her hand a squeeze, and I flew out of the ladies room in search of my photographer.

I found him, huddled around with the rest of the guys, and even though my mouth was dry and my head was racing, I casually told him we had to pack it up and head out. He looked a little surprised but shrugged and gathered up the gear. The instant we were out of hearing range of the other photographers, I told him what was up. His eyes flew open and his jaw dropped, but that only lasted an instant. This was news, *big* news, and he knew we were getting an exclusive.

We even went so far as tossing the equipment in the back of the truck and then pulling out of the lot, just to make sure the other news crews saw us leave. I was praying the woman wouldn't change her mind as we circled around and pulled to the rear of the building, then we dragged the gear back out and sneaked into the ladies room.

She was still there.

"It all began innocently," she explained in a voice choked with emotion.

The photographer was positioned behind her, taping past her back at me as I asked questions and listened to her heartrending response. She had accepted a date with a man who told her they were going to a fun party at a farm north of the city. After driving for more than an hour, he pulled off to a remote dirt road and reached for a bottle of whiskey.

"I panicked and asked him to take me home but he said, 'We're going to have some fun first. You're gonna meet my friends. They've been waiting for you.' "

I could feel shivers dancing up and down my spine, but I trained my face, knowing after all those years of studying colleagues that the reporter's job was to be serious and respectful, but keep tight control on personal emotions.

The young woman broke down sobbing then and it was all I could do not to cry with her as she went on to describe in painful and graphic detail how seven men appeared from the darkness, pulled her from the car and ripped off her clothing before taking turns raping her.

"They kept laughing and bragging about it the whole time."

The young woman concluded her terrible tale by explaining how the men then pushed her back into the car and one of them drove her to a main road and then ordered her to get out. She wandered in the dark, covered in blood and mud, until a passing motorist saw her and stopped.

"He took me to a hospital, and then they called the police."

I swallowed hard. "And why did you choose to tell your story?"

"To warn other young women in the audience. So it won't happen to them."

And that was it.

I wanted to cry and hug her and tell her everything was going to be okay, but I realized as a reporter, when someone has the courage to tell you a story like that, you have to have the courage to treat her with honor, not tears.

So I thanked her. And I wished her luck. I left her in that ladies room, and the photographer and I headed out to the van.

We didn't speak the entire way back to the station.

You'd have thought I'd been bursting to talk once we did get back, but I dragged my heels through the newsroom. I had to scrape up the nerve to tell the news director and my colleagues that I'd just scooped every other news reporter in town. I really didn't know what to expect. A hearty congratulations? A giant lecture on remembering my place?

I told the news director, and several of the reporters in the newsroom quickly got a whiff of what was going on. There was a moment of stunned silence — and then the excitement set in. *My* having the scoop also meant *our station* had the scoop, and everyone waited with great anticipation as the film was processed. Then we all gathered around during the edit and no one left that edit suite unaffected by the poignant story that unfolded.

That story led on the evening news that night, and eventually went on to win several awards, including another Golden Quill. It earned me the respect and the right to officially become Pittsburgh's first female general assignment news reporter.

After a decade of working — and a lifetime of dreaming — my big break had finally come. What thrilled me was the fact that I had been able to put all my skills to use, to not just prove to the big guys but prove *to myself* that I really did have what it takes to be a hard news reporter.

What sobered me was this new and full understanding of what the job truly entailed. It's called "hard news" for a reason.

Hearing it is hard. Seeing it is hard. For the victim, living it is hard. And for the reporter, telling it straight, getting it right, being fair to the viewer and fair to the victim, well . . . that's hard too.

I vowed to spend the rest of my career working hard to get hard news right.

▲ *Asleep at the Underwood*

4:30 PM | **with Hank Stohl**

NEW TIME!
5 to 6:15 PM

ADVENTURE TIME
with Paul Shannon

NEW NEWS!
6:15 to 6:30

ABC "EVENING REPORT"
PREMIERES TONIGHT

Top network news coverage featuring
on-the-spot news by John Cameron
Swayze, Bill Lawrence & Al Mann,
under the supervision of James Hag-
gerty

SAME TIME:
6:30 to 7

HIGHWAY PATROL
with Broderick Crawford

CLIMAXED BY
COMPLETE NEWS COVERAGE.

4 STAR
NEWS **7** P.M.

Pittsburgh's most up to the minute
NEWS with Carl Ide and Ed Conway,
followed by Eleanor Schano and the
weather. Then Dave Murray's news
documentary "Take 4"

More on 4
NOW BEGINNING OUR
4th GREAT YEAR

**WTAE
CHANNEL 4**

▲ *15 minute Network News, 15 minute Local News . . . expanded today to 3 hours*

5
The Only Chick in the Newsroom

*E*very day was a new adventure. As a general assignment news reporter, you never knew what the assignment manager would throw your way. One day it could be hard news — I covered murders, kidnappings, fatal fires — and the next day, I might find myself covering city politics or a trial in Federal Court. The day after that it could be Julian Bond or Princess Grace of Monaco. I was there for that famous moment when Soviet leader Nikita Khrushchev took off his shoe and pounded it on the table at the University of Pittsburgh's student union, showing his extreme displeasure over a reporter's question he didn't like. (I remember a big hole in the sole of Khrushchev's left shoe.) You name it, criminals, politicos, celebrities, I interviewed them all.

I even managed to snare a rare interview with Jackie Kennedy when JFK was campaigning in the West Virginia primary and made a whistle stop at the Twin Coaches — a nightclub in Belle

▲ *Eleanor interviewing Julian Bond*

Vernon, Pa. And once again, I found myself conducting an interview inside of a ladies room! I followed her in there, I admit it, and we chatted briefly before I asked if I could interview her on camera.

"About life on the campaign trail, kids, that kind of stuff," I assured her, since she'd made it pretty clear to the reporters outside that she would not be granting interviews. The impression I got was *here is a woman who is tired, tired of all the campaigning. Here is a woman who would much rather be spending time with her family without the glare of public scrutiny.* If she couldn't be with her family, I thought she might at least like to *talk* about them.

Jackie Kennedy agreed to the interview.

I brought the camera and photographer into the ladies room — there were no other women reporters so I knew we wouldn't be disturbed — and there Jackie granted an exclusive, which began by talking about the loss of an infant. We connected on that issue, and the more we talked, the more I was struck thinking what a paradox she was: A public figure regarded almost as American royalty, who at the moment seemed like just a regular working mom trying valiantly to juggle the realities of her family's life. What I remember most to this day is my surprise upon discovering that this statuesque beauty with such an incredibly regal appearance sounded like a little girl when she opened her mouth to speak. Her voice was a mere baby-doll melody as we chatted.

Jackie Kennedy wasn't the only interview I got because I connected to the subject on an elemental level as a woman. One thing I found out pretty fast: Some people felt more comfortable being interviewed and they would seek me out for exclusives. But I never *used* that angle intentionally to get a story. If subjects felt more comfortable being interviewed by a woman, if they perceived some kind of "motherly" persona in me, then that's *all* it was — *perception*. Because I set out to prove myself as a reporter and I'd been studying the best news guys in the business. I didn't take it easy on anyone. My goal was to get the story and get it right, and I was as tenacious as any of my male colleagues when it came to getting the facts.

All in all, I thought I was adjusting pretty well to life in the news room. And the other male reporters were adjusting very well *to me*, a constant presence before, but an equal now. Sure, they may have grumbled and muttered a few humorless jokes when it came time to shift the desks to accommodate the "chick in the news room," but they saw me working, knew the stories I was bringing back day after day, and they respected that.

The photographers quickly accepted me, too. We were together so closely that it wasn't long before few, if any, words even passed between us on the job. A glance, a crook of the finger, a nod of the head, and he was getting the shot I wanted, I was bee-lining for the subject we needed to interview. As reporters, we had to think on our feet, keep arranging and rearranging the story in our minds as more details unfolded on the scene, then we'd write the edit plans in the van on the way back to the station.

Grab it and run.

Get it and go.

It was exhilarating.

And then one day a story entered the newsroom that changed everything.

I had just finished doing the Noon news and returned to my desk outside the wire machine room. Wire machines regularly dispense bulletins from national news services, but since the non-stop clattering noise of the wire machines was so distracting, most news rooms — ours included — housed them in a glass cubicle. Every new intern was taught that one important duty was to clear the wire machines every 10 minutes or so. That meant that all the new copy had to be scanned and "hooked," separating news as local, national, international, etc. It was a routine task unless some breaking story occurred.

The urgency of a news story moving on the wires was signaled by a series of ringing bells. One bell, big news…two bells, very big news . . . 3 , 4 and 5 bells, news of urgent importance.

On that particular day, a young intern made his normal check of the wire machines but apparently paid no attention to the bells signaling a news bulletin of extreme urgency. Instead, he ripped off the paper and nonchalantly tossed it on the desk of the editor on duty.

In a matter-of-fact voice he announced, "By the way, President Kennedy got shot."

John F. Kennedy, the 35th President of the United States of America, had been mortally wounded during a motorcade procession in Dallas, Texas.

Only six of us sat in the newsroom at the moment but I remember we all stared at each other in stunned silence. This was not just news; this was a defining moment in American history.

A heartbeat later, chaos erupted. Paul Long grabbed the bulletin and ran to the studio. A news bulletin slide was already on the screen interrupting normal programming. The phone lines started lighting up and the harried receptionist, Irene, reported that irate viewers were calling to complain that their favorite soap opera was being interrupted.

Within seconds, the saturation news coverage began, and lasted for many days afterward. The wall to wall coverage was handled by the networks: ABC, NBC and CBS. The most memorable of the anchors was CBS newsman Walter Cronkite, who read the wire service newsflash that alerted many Americans to the tragedy: "From Dallas, Texas. . . apparently official: President Kennedy died at 1 p.m. (CST)—2:00 EST, some 38 minutes ago."

This usually unflappable anchor had to pause while reading to choke back his tears.

Our local newsroom became a scene of commotion and confusion. Something happened that left the entire staff speechless. In the midst of the biggest story of the century our boss, the news director, left town. That's right. He just walked out with the explanation that he had made a prior commitment to drive his mother-in-law to Michigan for the weekend. Nothing stopped him, not even the assassination of the President of the United States.

The rest of the staff rallied and just started making executive decisions to cover the news and serve the viewer. I wanted desperately to be part of this moment in history, and was determined to deliver reports from Washington, D.C. The body of the President would be flown back to lie in state in the Capitol Rotunda. My husband and I gathered our two little girls and headed to Washington in our old "woody" station wagon. I would file audio reports for the next several days that were aired on both our TV station and the sister radio station. Although Jennifer and Lorie were quite young, they do have a dim memory of the drama that unfolded before the eyes of a bereaved nation.

▲ *Lorie, Warren, Eleanor, Jennifer*

Do I regret blending my dual roles as mother and reporter at that event? No, I do not. I think my daughters grew up with a healthy, age-appropriate awareness that a world existed outside of their own cozy home. I never consciously "brought my work home with me" but my work, after all, was news, and news happened everywhere, at any time.

As I covered the hard news, my work hours, like the stories, got tougher. So I, like many working mothers, tried to overcompensate for the time spent away from my kids by volunteering to serve on every committee at the girls' school, produce cupcakes for every bake sale, lead activities for the Brownie troop. It was a balancing act that left me breathless and exhausted but it did work for my daughters and that made me happy.

I think it's a lot easier to raise children when they are very young, frankly. You pick them up, you cart them around. Once they get older, once they enter school, it's a barrage of scheduling, who needs to be where when, which existed even back then — although in comparison to today's Soccer Mom syndrome, some may believe the 1960's were "simpler times." Maybe for some, but not for me.

When cataloging my career for a resume, I note many broadcast "firsts." But I was experiencing a personal "first" too, one that wasn't talked about so openly in the mid-1960's: My marriage was slowly falling apart. I don't even think "falling apart" is the right phrase, because there were no arguments, no outward signs that anything was wrong. It may sound strange but the children never heard either one of us raise our voices.

I'd say my marriage to Warren had become "sanitized," for lack of a better word. It seemed the only thing we shared anymore was a common love for our children. Also, I was working hard, not just for the love of the job but also to help support the family. After awhile, I just lost respect for a man who was willing to let his wife shoulder most of the responsibility of providing for the family while he was pursuing various interests, whether they paid a decent salary or not.

But even that wasn't all of it. There's never one simple reason, no formula to explain how a couple can suddenly wake up one morning and look each other in the eye and ask, "Who are you?"

It happened to us, though, so in 1967 I made a decision: I told Warren I wanted a divorce.

It was painful, for Warren and for me. And there were points of feeling terribly guilty, too, because of our daughters. *What about staying together for the children's sake?* Isn't that the reason so many people give for staying in a bad marriage? Sure, I wish we all could have lived *happily ever after*, but I didn't see that ever happening, and I didn't want my children to grow up in that atmosphere of mere tolerance and cool, polite behavior. Children *do* sense that kind of thing, and I didn't want my girls to grow up thinking that's what a relationship should be like.

Don't get me wrong, divorce is not something I take lightly. I don't condone it, but I don't condemn it, either. I think it takes courage to end a marriage and looking back, I cannot say that I regret the decision. In my humble opinion, it is much better to end a relationship than to carry it on for a lifetime of indifference.

I only wish my *parents* understood my rationale. My decision to get a divorce sent shockwaves rocketing through my parents *and* my brother and sister. I was the first family member in a long line of strict Catholics ever to get a divorce, and in my parents' eyes, it was nothing short of a family disgrace. In 1967, there was a terrible reputation attached to "divorcee." My brother said he would never speak to me again, and he didn't for a very long time.

I soldiered on, hoping they would come around to understand my decision, but there were petty and not-so-petty details to work out as part of the divorce, and my parents witnessed them with tight-lipped disapproval. Thankfully, my daughters were spared the details of the separation. I was forced to pay the equity in our home to their father so we could remain in the house the girls had grown up in, but I muddled through because I believed a "good divorce" would set a better example for them than a "bad marriage."

Then, shortly after our divorce, Warren remarried, to a woman who had two boys the exact same ages as our daughters. He insisted that if Jennifer and Lorie were to see him that it had to be at his new family's residence. The girls were very upset each time they came home from those visits until one night they walked in the door crying, "We don't want to go to Daddy's house ever again."

▲ *Dad and Mom*

Me and Mom celebrating our July birthdays ▶

▲ *Eleanor's First Communion. Back row Grandma & Grandpap Daley, Dad, Mom & Brother Bob*

Lorie and Jennifer — off to Mass on Easter Sunday

Jennifer and Lorie - sisters all grown up now but still best friends

Jack and Eleanor riding, hiking, biking, boating

A day in Venice following a bike trip through the Veneto region of northern Italy

I was crushed. I wanted them to spend time with their father, but as often as I tried to explain to Warren that the present arrangement wasn't working and that he could see the girls anytime, anywhere *except* at his new home, the plea fell on deaf ears.

"They feel like outsiders when they come to your new home," I told him, then begged, "Pick a neutral location for your visits. The girls don't feel comfortable with your step-children and your new wife yet."

Warren's reply was straightforward and brief. "No. I have a new family now and if the girls want to become part of it, fine. If not, I suppose I won't be able to see them."

And that's what happened. Years went by and even though we all lived only a few miles apart there were no attempts at a reunion. What a tragedy that a father gave up the opportunity to see his beautiful little daughters mature into accomplished young ladies, and later, extraordinary adults.

I wish I could say that was the end of it, but it wasn't. Warren even fought child support payments — all the way to the Pennsylvania Supreme Court. The landmark decision handed down stands to this day. The court ruled in *his* favor — stating that if a woman is capable of earning a living, a man need only provide minimal support, which in this case was $135 a month for both children.

Warren is gone now, and how I wish he had left a different legacy to his daughters, but my girls and I survived. We became a team, just the three of us, and we carved out a new dynamic that continues to this day, a bond no one can ever break.

With time, the pain and confusion of the divorce began to ease, and I *did* start to get used to the feeling of flying solo. I was working hard, totally absorbed in the lives of my daughters and in the progress of my career.

I was in no hurry to start dating again, but being in the public eye on television every night left me with no loss of attention

from men. I had plenty of invitations from decent gentlemen —
and even some invitations from not-so-decent men, often
married, who thought they could reel me in with that 'irresistible'
pick-up line, "I have a big news scoop for you. I'll tell you about
it over drinks and dinner."

I declined them all.

The truth was, I hadn't dated in more than a dozen years and
just the thought of having to start all over again, making small
talk, trying to appear interested and charming, was just too big a
chore. I already worked with some of the most interesting and
powerful men in broadcasting, and they filled my life with good,
intelligent conversation.

WTAE was an ABC affiliate station and so it was common for
some of the network reporters to visit the local stations, and they
were enjoyable contacts, too. Why would I need to simper and
smile to impress some date when network science editor Jules
Bergman was exchanging ideas with me at the office, or Peter
Jennings was popping by to chat? In fact, Peter Jennings made
his way through Pittsburgh several times a year and he and I
struck up a friendship. I even think of it as an intimate
friendship, although not in the usual sense of that word. It was
intimate in the *human* sense, when someone touches your life
and affects the way you move forward.

In early November, 1967, just months after my divorce, I
took my daughters to work (as I often did; they still enjoyed
sitting in the audience for the 5 p.m. Paul Shannon show) and we
had just stepped into the lunchroom for a snack when Peter
Jennings came in. My girls never knew he was a big star; he was
just a nice man they bumped into on occasion who was kind and
funny. There we all sat, munching on those bright orange peanut
butter and cheese crackers, in the lunchroom of WTAE.

He was great with the kids — spoke their language — and
since it was November he casually asked, "Have you girls ever
been to the Macy's Thanksgiving Day Parade?" Jennifer shook

her head no; Lorie explained that we always watched it on TV. Peter leaned in close and said in a big, mock-whisper, "If your mom will bring you to New York, I will take you to the Macy's parade."

The girls launched into a full-scale assault. *"Can we go? Can we go? Pleeeeeeeease, can we go?!"*

I finally relented. It was our first holiday post-divorce and I thought the change of scenery would do the girls good.

We flew to New York and true to his word, Peter Jennings showed up at our hotel early on Thanksgiving morning with a car. I'm sure he could have taken us to some VIP box to view the parade but that wasn't his style. He took us to the perfect spot along the parade route, where we stood and watched as each float came by, enthralled by a running commentary from the most respected and eloquent journalist I have ever known. Later, he insisted we all go to Rockefeller Center for hot chocolate, and before he left he escorted us to the giant toy store FAO Schwartz, where he bought each of my girls a souvenir. Throughout the day, Peter regaled Jennifer and Lorie with stories of places he had been and how other people live around the world. He was a teacher who wanted children to understand the news.

He and I frequently discussed the broadcasting industry and I will always remember a lesson he taught *to me*. He'd been put into the network anchor chair at ABC at the tender age of 27, and he confided in me that even though Lady Luck had smiled on him, he'd felt he wasn't ready for the task. He put it to me this way: *"Luck is where preparation meets opportunity, and I was given the opportunity before I was really prepared."*

I got the message: Sink or swim. I had always done that in my career, and I knew now that I had to dive back in and do that in my personal life.

Peter Jennings' death on August 7, 2005, left a hole in American journalism that will not be easily filled. It also left a

Eleanor Schano

ELEANOR SCHAN
WIIC-TV

LOOK 4-WARD TO
4 STAR NEWS

MON.-FRI. 7 P. M.

Publicity photographs as I rode the airwaves all over town.

From one great team to another...

GET 'EM BUC

SPORTS
SAM NOVER

ACTION LINE
ELEANOR SCHANO

WEATHER
DON RIGGS

hole in my soul, for the memory of a broadcast legend who took the time to narrate a parade for two little girls, and counsel a friend at a critical time in her life.

* * *

I loved the atmosphere of the newsroom at WTAE. Oh, I wasn't unaffected by the *news* — it was a news reporter's lot in life to compartmentalize emotions as the bad stuff happened — but the room itself, the pace, the constant tapping of typewriters, created an energy that reminds me of the way you feel at the end of a particularly thrilling roller coaster ride. It was exhilarating.

And if the *room* had the atmosphere of a thrill ride, the *people* I worked with had the attitude of thrill-seekers. These guys were amazing, and intense.

There was Herb Morrison, the News Coordinator, whose lasting fame was as the newsman on the scene when the Hindenburg crashed in 1937. Dave Murray was a brilliant, no-nonsense guy who also appeared on camera at the end of the evening news to deliver biting commentary called "Take Four," where he proved himself a formidable on-air presence. George Thomas had the toughest job, if you ask me. He was the Assignment Manager, and it was his duty to monitor the police radio and take in all the information of breaking stories. Every station wanted the "big scoop" and it was George's responsibility to dispatch crews and make sure the stories were back and edited in time for air.

My desk was in a small office adjacent to the main news room. There were only three desks, ones for News Reporter Carl Ide and Sports Director Ed Conway on one side of the room, and then a little desk pushed up against a file cabinet for me on the other side. Working in such close proximity made us all very good friends very fast.

Carl was a good guy, your typical dogged newsman. Ed Conway was like a magnet. When he entered the room, people were just drawn to him, to his broad smile and easy personality.

Like I said, I was in no way *looking* for a new romantic relationship, but isn't that always the way things work? When you least expect it, things just happen.

One night, Ed and I walked to the parking lot together after work and he said, "Hey, if you're not doing anything tomorrow night, would you like to grab some dinner?"

I didn't think too hard about my reply. Immediately, I said, "Sure, why not." Ed was divorced, so was I, and I already knew him well as a friend and colleague. Dinner with Ed would be an easy, comfortable experience.

The next night, we went to a small diner close to the station. Ed had to be back for the 11 p.m. newscast and I had to get home. As I had thought, dinner with Ed was easy and comfortable.

It was almost too easy.

We'd been good friends for such a long time, and we had so much in common, we knew the same people, understood each other's work, that we totally skipped that awkward part at the start of a relationship where you have to sift through details to find out if you're right for each other. Ed and I *were* right for each other, and our relationship was one that just evolved, a good place for both of us to be at that point in our lives.

Ed was the Sports Director, so he frequented the ballparks and I would go with him when I could squeeze it into my schedule. He was well-respected and greatly admired, and Ed's genuine love of the game was contagious — strong enough to convert *me* into a hockey fan when he became the voice of the Pittsburgh Penguins! I went to 68 hockey games in one season! Ed also was the voice of the University of Pittsburgh's Panther football team, so I sat in the bleachers with Rosette Hillgrove, the wife of Ed's play-by-play color announcer, Bill Hillgrove.

Working together while we dated didn't prove to be any big deal. We kept it low-key at the office, and since we already had a rhythm for working together it was no big chore to make this fit.

The only fly in the proverbial ointment was the new News Director. This new guy had a reputation in the industry as someone with a bad mouth and a worse temper. People just wanted to stay out of his way.

I tried that tactic, too, but as the only woman in the newsroom, it was hard to blend in. He was the kind of guy who would call me into his office, close the door, and make snide remarks about my clothing, "assessing" my on-camera appearance in a vulgar and way-too-personal way, if you know what I mean.

The Women's Movement was still in its infancy and any talk of equal rights and sexual harassment was a whisper on the wind, so I did what most women of the day were forced to do if they wanted to keep their jobs. I deflected it as best I could, and accepted the disgusting episodes in tight-lipped silence.

Oh, he wasn't the *only* one who still thought of the women in the business as hood ornaments. I had a sales manager who thought it was okay to ask me to walk down the hall slowly so he could check out my legs and even once he attempted to pat my back end as I passed by. (I put an end to that fast by mentioning that I knew his *wife* quite well and thought it was time she and I had a nice, long chat about hubby's behavior.)

Even some of the cameramen got a little freaky at times, shooting close-ups of women's breasts and bottoms so they could take them back to the video room for a little impromptu "snuff party."

Lovely, huh?

It was useless to complain to the news room boss, because he was more disgusting than the rest of them put together! Still, I made it known what I thought of those kinds of antics, until I developed a reputation for being too easily offended, and the nickname *Miss Goody Two Shoes*.

Some of the men I interviewed were no better. A few days before Christmas, I covered a story with a top political figure. When I entered his office, he pulled out a Santa hat from his desk drawer and tried to yank me into his arms, asking if I wanted to "sit on Santa's lap."

Then there was one incident that may have been exacerbated because I was a woman, but was instigated mostly because I was a member of the media.

We were living in turbulent times. During the race riots of the 1960's we had our share of conflicts locally. The growing push by African Americans to crack the building trades unions had reached a head in Pittsburgh, Pennsylvania. It was the week before Labor Day in 1969 and the city was shaken by five successive days of demonstrations by African Americans, and counter-demonstrations by white construction workers. Pittsburgh police were totally unprepared for the violence that erupted, and we reported that fact just as we reported every other one associated with the story. The Pittsburgh Police were not happy.

The Black Construction Coalition called for a mass demonstration at the new sports stadium under construction (Three Rivers) on Pittsburgh's North Side. The objective was to shut down construction and along with dozens of other news reporters I found myself in the middle of a melee that broke out.

My reports appeared on the evening news and even though I made an effort to keep my 9 and 10 year old daughters from watching they learned from their classmates that their mother was in the midst of what appeared to be a "battleground," and all I could do was try to explain the situation in a way that would make my daughters more sensitive than their classmates.

The situation continued to approach its boiling point when Nate Smith, one of about 125 Black men in a union of 7,000 members, showed up to cool the tensions. He recruited many of the men there into what became known as Operation Dig, a training program that ultimately resulted in 90 Black men being trained as operating engineers holding union cards and eligible for union jobs. Operation Dig was later praised as one of the best programs of its kind, and Nate Smith became a hero.

Even though the demonstrations ended, the tension between members of the media and police continued. But I wasn't even thinking about that early one foggy morning in October, 1969.

Jennifer and Lorie had overslept and missed the school bus to St. Simon & Jude school. It was only a five minute ride from our house and, as I had done many times before, I threw on a robe over my pj's and drove them to school. I took a shortcut on the way home, taking a seldom-used secondary road. I remember the fog was so thick as I turned the corner that I could barely make out the image of a police squad car parked at the side of the road.

Even though I was driving at the speed limit and following all the rules of the road, I heard a siren and saw the flashing lights of the squad behind me, ordering me to stop.

I rolled down my window and politely asked the officer what was wrong. He ordered me to turn off the ignition and get out of the car. It just didn't seem like the right thing to do, especially since I was wearing a tattered pink chenille bathrobe. But, more than that I knew the circumstances that had created strained relations between some members of the Pittsburgh Police force and television reporters, and from the smug grin on his face it was clear he knew who I was. I thought I'd be safer if I just stayed in my car.

I asked him again why I was being stopped and he said something about my tires crossing the center line — an interesting call since the secondary road we were on *did not have a center line painted on it*. Then he pushed me back and reached in to grab the car keys from the ignition. He even took off his helmet and banged it against the roof of my car while ordering me again to get out of the vehicle.

I was willing myself not to panic, but then he grabbed my arm and yanked hard, clearly intending to drag me from the car, and I screamed, "Stop! Leave me alone!" swatting at his hand where his fingers dug into my skin.

What he did next was unthinkable. He reached for his two-way radio and yelled, "Officer in trouble, officer in trouble!"

Just in case you don't know, that is the call when an officer is in imminent danger, say if a criminal pulls a gun on him, and it is guaranteed to get an immediate response from every nearby officer.

Our tussle continued for a few brief seconds before a swarm of squad cars surrounded my vehicle. The police canine division or corp even showed up!

I was arrested and put into a paddy wagon and taken to #1 police station in downtown Pittsburgh, where I was charged with disorderly conduct. As fate would have it, a cub reporter from the *Pittsburgh Press* was there to witness this humiliation and capture the moment for all time on film. My picture appeared that evening with the story caption "Eleanor Schano charged with disorderly conduct." Since the incident took place in the very early morning, I was certain many readers would think I was just coming *home* from a wild night on the town instead of simply heading home after driving my kids to school.

The ugly saga ended when Police Chief John Kelly learned of the incident. He immediately got all charges against me dropped.

To my knowledge that is the only time I *became* the story instead of reporting it, but television is a funny business. As traumatic as it was at the time, once you're back in the newsroom your colleagues kind of view it as a badge of honor, and so the whole episode blew over fast enough.

What *didn't* blow over was the disgusting News Director's continued harassment. There was always some kind of crude comment, some innuendo, until one day, I came to what is commonly referred to as "the straw that breaks the camel's back." The very disgusting News Director called me into his office with what he was certain would be a *fabulous* feature that could appear weekly on the Friday night news.

"You and I can go out *together* and cover the big entertainment events, charity balls, theatre openings, things like that," he announced grandly. "I'll even buy a tux so I can escort you in style. We'll have a *blast!*"

It was the kind of moment where bile actually rises in your throat and you start to shake. It went beyond insulting, beyond rude. It was an affront to my dignity, and it was the one time in my career I allowed my emotions to rule.

I raced up the three flights of steps to the General Manager's office and tossed out an ultimatum: *He goes or I go.*

The GM squirmed. "Eleanor, you're putting me in a very difficult position. Go home, think it over. Come back when you've calmed down."

So that was it, I thought as I left his office. I'd been at WTAE since 1958. I loved my job. I loved the people. I loved being able to work with Ed Conway every day. But I was enraged.

So I headed back the next day and handed in a letter of resignation.

I had no trouble finding another job. Within weeks, I received a phone call from Byron "By" Williams, the News Director at WIIC-TV (which would later become WPXI-TV). By was a heads-up, straight-forward, no-nonsense kind of guy I'd known for years, and I knew he wouldn't tolerate any kind of funny stuff in his shop.

The job would be as Action Line Reporter. It was an ombudsman position, advocacy journalism, the chance to use the

ELEANOR SCHANO
JOINS BOGUT
AND SCHAUGHENCY
MORNINGS ON KDKA RADIO

Eleanor Schano, well known Pittsburgh broadcast personality has joined the morning team of Jack Bogut and Ed Schaughency 6-10 AM; Monday through Friday on KDKA Radio.

Eleanor, a twenty-four year veteran of broadcast journalism, has received the Golden Quill Award three times for outstanding news coverage.

Eleanor handles the 6:30 AM and 8:30 AM newscasts as well as morning traffic reports. She also contributes to KDKA's "90 to 6" newscasts 4:30 to 6 PM weekdays.

KDKA RADIO 1020 GROUP W

▲ *Once again, I was the only female in the newsroom surrounded by such titans as Ed Schaughency and Jack Bogut*

power of the medium to help people who needed a voice louder than their own to take on anyone from government bureaucrats to utility companies and corporate bigwigs. I knew what it was like to be in the minority, to be the one trying valiantly to be heard, so the sense of justice attached to the Action Line job appealed to me. I accepted and started a few days later.

The ironic post-script to this story is that just a month after that, the disgusting News Director from WTAE got into a major blow-out with the General Manager, and was literally chased out of the building and told he wasn't even allowed to return to pick up his belongings!

But I don't regret the strange twist of fate that took me to WIIC, because in no time at all I settled in as Action Line Reporter, and soon we were averaging 500 requests for help a week. It was a tough task to sort through the stories of injustice and helplessness and only be able to do one story a day. The desperation in people's voices haunted me. There was a single mother of six left homeless following eviction. . . the amputee who needed a wheelchair. Every day it was more pain and sorrow, and I took my job home with me in a way that I hadn't before.

At night my daughters would help me pick out stories that most needed coverage. They learned a lot about caring and compassion and they helped pulled me through.

I wasn't complaining. There were no other female feature reporters and it would be many years before the other station would add female news reporters to their staffs. Still, I was anxious to move forward but there was no other place for me to go except that news anchor desk, and that just wasn't going to happen. The anchor desk was the sole domain of white males.

In addition to the job itself, the new cast of characters, a.k.a. colleagues, in the newsroom made me comfortable and happy to head into work each day. Local legends such as Ray Tannehill, Adam Lynch, and Sam Nover were my new pals. It wasn't the same as sharing an office with Ed Conway, but it was fun and they were great.

It had been three years since my divorce and re-marriage was not high on my list of priorities, but Ed and I continued to date and develop a wonderful relationship, the kind that is both comfortable and extraordinary at the same time. When Ed proposed in the spring of 1970, I hesitated just long enough to consider all the evidence: The most important thing to me was that my daughters Jennifer and Lorie were truly fond of Ed. And I loved him. Those two factors combined were pretty compelling.

I told Ed yes.

When Sam Nover — WIIC's sports reporter — learned that I was marrying WTAE Sports Director Ed Conway, he marched right into the General Manager's office and blustered about a conflict of interest.

"I am not going to have someone who is *sleeping with the competition* working with me every day!"

I couldn't blame Sam. Sports is a competitive business and the name of the game is to get the exclusive story. . . although I had to laugh at the image of myself as some kind of newsroom *Mata Hari*, sneaking info about the big game to my husband over pillow talk!

Ed and I were professionals so we knew there was only one right thing to do: We vowed *never* to discuss our professional lives at home. I said as much to Sam, telling him, "I do solemnly swear never to take work home with me. You have to trust my word."

Sam did trust me and I never once broke my pledge.

It was smooth sailing after that. Ed and I married on June 30, 1970.

Everyone loved Ed. His movie star good looks made him look more like a matinee idol than a sportscaster . . . a fact that was not lost on women who lavished him with attention everywhere we went. But his looks weren't the only thing that made Ed stand out in a crowd. His Irish wit meant his stories and anecdotes were punctuated with humor, charm, and good deal of self-deprecation. Ed loved to laugh at himself.

He won over my parents, my siblings (my brother was talking to me again after the whole divorce disgrace), all of my friends. And my daughters adored him. Where I was strict, Ed was the "fun one." He was lenient and generous in handing out allowances even if the girls hadn't finished their chores. Lorie was a big sports fan and Ed often would smuggle her on the plane and take her to Pirates Spring Training Camp in Ft. Myers, Florida. We all went to Steeler games, hockey games, basketball games. . . you name the sport, and we'd all be there! You definitely get the VIP treatment when you're one of the three TV Sports Directors in town, so we were mixing with local media, network honchos, and even the players themselves.

These were good times, *great* times, wildly in love, happy as a family, and both Ed and I working in television with all the enthusiasm and dedication of people on their way up the ladder.

I was at the end of my 30's but that looming Big 4-0 didn't bother me in the least. I was comfortable with who I was, and where I was. What was getting a little *un*comfortable though was the Action Line Reporter job. I was getting burned out by all of the sadness and I secretly hoped something else would come along, something within the station that would allow me to make a shift. Who could have guessed that good ol' Uncle Sam would be the one to provide me with that opportunity!

It was the early 1970's so Affirmative Action was the theme spreading through the broadcasting industry. Stations were threatened with the loss of their FCC licenses if they didn't create more visible roles for women and people of color. Still, imagine how flabbergasted I was when WIIC approached me with the offer to become *a news anchor!*

I would be the first solo female news anchor in Pittsburgh, certainly *one* of the first nationwide. You bet I told them yes!

My desk was moved from the bullpen into the hallowed space reserved for anchormen — now referred to as "anchor *persons*." The office was cramped, with drab gray walls and stained carpeting. It had a distinct odor to it, too, a combination of stale coffee, cigarette smoke, and Ray Tannehill's Aramis cologne. We even had a resident contingency of vermin, which meant the whole space was nicely appointed with mousetraps. It was dingy, deplorable, and I absolutely *loved* it!

The guys accepted me as an equal, and we regularly argued over headlines and lead stories. Should our top story be the fatal car crash on Route 51, or the water main break that left 2,000 residents high and dry? Do we go with the growing trend toward *if-it-bleeds-it-leads* journalism, or do we stick with the facts and tell the stories that matter most? (We chose the stories that mattered most.)

It wasn't glamorous; it was downright gritty. I labored away for the sake of the viewers, but there were times when I also made it personal so my own daughters could reap some benefits from my professional experience.

Jennifer and Lorie were teenagers now, a fierce and frightening new frontier in the 1970's, believe me, but I vowed to keep them on the straight and narrow. Drugs and alcohol were everywhere. We would talk for hours about the dangers of giving in to temptation and I often used the scare tactic to remind them of the consequences of breaking the law. I arranged with the help of the Greentree Police Chief to have them observe a drug bust and the subsequent arrests. The three of us sat in an ante room as seven of their friends were brought in one by one, fingerprinted and posing for mug shots. They never forgot that night or that lesson.

Then there was the time I decided to expose what was happening during the many rock and roll concerts that were performed at the Civic Arena (now Mellon Arena).

The rock era was in full swing and Jennifer and Lorie begged to be allowed to attend concerts. *No way were my kids going to be exposed to what was happening!* I thought. I had seen the video brought back by our news photographers and I was appalled. Parents would drop off their children without realizing what was going on inside. There was not enough security to handle the thousands of kids who were running wild in what I can only describe as smoke-filled, blanket-strewn chaos.

Wasn't this my opportunity to use the power of the medium to focus attention on what was clearly becoming a serious problem? I had to get the attention of a prominent public official if I wanted to get something done, so I called Tom Foerster, the Chairman of the Allegheny County Commissioners, and invited him to join me and my cameraman at the Alice Cooper — Blood Rocks concert. For those of you fortunate enough to have missed this era, Cooper was famous for his on-stage antics, which included mock-hangings, guillotines, movie monsters, gallons of fake blood, and throwing live chickens into the crowd. And that was *tame* compared to the action happening in the audience! It was the "biggest pot party and love-in" in town.

Fortunately, Commissioner Foerster brought along the Fire Marshall to witness the situation gone out-of-control. My story that night was the lead on the 11 p.m. news and it sent shockwaves through the community. It also resulted in the enforcement of existing laws and created new stricter guidelines that governed all rock concerts from that night forward.

My image in the public eye might have been enhanced by the report, but my image on the Mommy track at home was knocked down a notch or two. After all, what teen wants her mom to be a snitch and blow the whistle ending all the fun?

I guess I was still *Miss Goody Two Shoes*, but the guys at WIIC never teased me about it in a nasty way. And thankfully, they never changed their own behavior just because "a lady was present." It made me feel good that they considered me "just one of the guys."

I'll never forget the night back in 1971 when the Pittsburgh Pirates were in the play-offs for the World Series. That night, I wasn't the only one treated to a display of colorful language!

The game was in extra innings and we all sat in the newsroom waiting to go on the air when Bob Moose threw a wild pitch that ended the game in defeat.

We all rushed up the ramp to the studio for the news, my co-anchor Adam Lynch and me several steps behind sportscaster Jan Hutchins.

"Wow," Jan mused, "that was a pretty shitty way to lose a ballgame. How about if I say that on the air tonight?"

Adam Lynch shrugged and laughed, "Sure, why not?"

But Jan didn't quite get the message that Adam was joking, because that's the way he led off the newscast: "What a shitty way to lose a ballgame."

We cut to break immediately and News Director By Williams bolted into the studio. "Did I hear what I think I heard?"

Jan got a pretty severe reprimand for that one, but when it came to colorful language, I have to hand the All Time All-Star Award to our sports reporter, Sam Nover.

Everyone marveled at the way Sam could use the same four-letter word as a noun, pronoun, preposition, and adjective — all in the same sentence! The more I'd wince, the more expletives he muttered, always with a smile and a wink at me — and one day he even brought me a recording of comedian George Carlin's *Seven Words You Can't Say on TV.*

One Friday afternoon, just minutes before we had to head into the studio to deliver the news, I decided it was high time to shock ol' Sam, so in a voice just loud enough for him to hear, I leaned over and said, "Don't forget your F*!@#iKING script."

He did indeed look shocked, and then immediately responded with his characteristic quick wit, "Eleanor, if you're going to use the F-word, you must have the right body language, and I just don't think you'll ever pull it off." He was right. I never did let my language degenerate, and I never did convince Sam to improve his, but the whole episode sticks out in my mind because it represents a story I once heard about the recipe for being a successful woman:

Look like a lady. . .
Think like a man . . .
Act like a woman . . .
And work like a dog.

***

During the summer of 1973, I began to notice that my husband Ed was slowing down. He complained of being tired — very uncharacteristic for this bubbly and energetic man — and he also said he was having difficulty swallowing. No amount of coaxing could get him to see a doctor, not even when he started to noticeably lose weight. I prayed for some kind of intervention, that someone other than myself would have the courage to confront Ed about his health, and my prayers were answered in the form of Dr. Joe Finegold, the Pittsburgh Pirates team physician.

We were attending a banquet one evening and I was seated between Joe and Ed. By now, there was a noticeable change in Ed's appearance. The once incredibly handsome man with a widows peak that made women swoon was pale and drawn. He did manage to keep that trademark dazzling smile of his, which he used to shrug off Dr. Finegold's insistence that Ed come into the office for an exam.

"Sure, doc. . . just as soon as the season's over."

As any sports fan knows, the "season" is never over. Baseball runs into football which runs into basketball which runs into hockey which runs into baseball. . . It just never ends.

By the end of October, Ed could barely keep up with his schedule of pre-game reports, post-game interviews, and press conferences. He was exhausted and finally agreed to make an appointment to see Dr. Finegold. It didn't take long for the test results to come back.

Cancer of the esophagus. Prognosis, not good.

We made the rounds of the top oncologists in Pittsburgh but the word was always the same: Terminal cancer.

Ed Conway was just 48 years old. How could this be?

I was devastated but I just refused to give up hope. And for awhile, it even seemed like his strength was picking up. He continued to work on air at WTAE — rarely missing a newscast, and for a time, he even seemed to be in a state of denial, making long-range future plans for adventurous family vacations.

I kept up my own schedule at WIIC, and fought the exhaustion that went along with work, parenting, escorting Ed to doctor appointments, and all-consuming worry. Byron Williams was a great friend and a great boss, an ex-Marine with a nose for news and the ability to manage a stable of egomaniacal news reporters at the same time. He understood my struggle to honor work commitments and still be there to support Ed and raise my kids, and for that I will be forever grateful.

It was early May when we were offered a glimmer of hope. Doctors thought maybe they could operate and buy Ed some more time. We agreed and the surgery was a success. He was recovering nicely in Presbyterian Hospital.

For many long hours, I sat by Ed's side, anguished by how hard it was for him simply to summon the strength to speak. Cancer may have ravaged his body but not his spirit. In a voice that was weak and hoarse, Ed would ask when doctors thought he might go home, or he'd say how much he looked forward to "getting back to work." Ed was optimistically looking forward to recuperating over the summer and being back on the air before Pitt football season started in the fall.

One afternoon, Ed's attention was caught by a voice in the hallway and he managed to rasp out, "Sounds like Billy Hillgrove."

Bill Hillgrove had been Ed's color commentator for the Pitt Panther football games for so many years and was a sports reporter at WTAE TV. Now their paths were crossing on the 8th floor of Presbyterian hospital. Bill's father-in-law was also fighting terminal cancer of the esophagus, and he was in the room right next to Ed.

During Ed's illness, Bill Hillgrove had taken over as interim sports director at Channel 4. He would listen with empathy as I released my grief and once, in a choked and emotional voice, he told me, "I always wanted to be a TV sports anchor, but not now . . . not like this. . ."

We all clung to the hope that a miracle would present itself. To me, a "miracle" would have been more time, just a little more time, before the inevitable end.

On May 26th, I had just finished the 6 p.m. news and went to the hospital to find that By Williams and his wife Jeanne had stopped in to visit. We all noticed that Ed seemed a bit disoriented. I was due back at the station to do the 11 p.m. news, but By said he and Jeanne would stay at the hospital until I got back.

Ed was sleeping when I left.

A couple of hours later, I was unhooking my microphone just moments after the newscast finished, when a desk assistant came running into the studio to say there was an urgent call from the hospital. I stumbled blindly to the phone and heard a voice on the other end say, "I'm sorry to tell you, your husband has suffered an episode and I think you should get here as quickly as possible."

An "episode?" I had no idea what that was supposed to mean but I was totally unprepared for what I found when I returned to the hospital. Ed's bed was empty.

I saw a nurse approaching. She took me gently by the arm and said she'd escort me to the cardiac intensive care unit. I walked with her like it was a dream — or a nightmare. When I got to the ICU, By and Jeanne were standing inside the door. They explained to me that without any warning Ed had gone into cardiac arrest. The code blue alert was sounded and Ed was put on life-support before being transferred to the ICU.

I stayed there all night watching him breathe in and out, the wispy, swishy sound of the life-support constant and unnerving.

Ed's color looked good, his face looked peaceful. I kept telling myself that he looked better than he had in a long time, and that he could pull through this.

At daybreak I went home and fell into a deep, exhausted sleep. A ringing phone roused me out of it and a nurse on the other end was telling me that I should be back at the hospital by 10 a.m. for a meeting with the doctors.

"What kind of meeting?"

"There are important things to talk about. We'd rather not go into detail until you're here."

All these vague and disjointed terms were getting on my nerves. An *episode*? A *meeting*? About *important things*?

Fatigue had dulled my ability to process any of it and I was operating purely on auto-pilot when I pulled my car back into the hospital lot. I have never felt as alone as I did that morning

— ushered into a tiny conference room to find six doctors in white coats all crammed around the table.

"There has been a brain death," one of the doctors announced.

I didn't respond. I *couldn't* respond. Fear and grief and confusion surrounded me like a brick wall. So the doctor tried again.

With no emotion at all in his voice, he repeated, "Your husband has suffered a brain death and we need you to make a decision."

Keep in mind the year was 1974 and the issue of life support was not yet brought into the public arena. Back in those days, no one talked about living wills or do-not-resuscitate orders. "Brain death" was not a commonly talked about term. Besides, Ed was young — just 48 — so we'd never thought there was a need to discuss end-of-life issues yet.

I had no idea what "decision" they were talking about. And no one offered an explanation.

I had to ask, and my voice sounded foreign in my own ears. "What kind of decision do you want me to make?"

"You have to tell us when to pull the plug."

Pull the plug?

"But Ed is doing fine," I stammered. "His color is good. Just give him time."

"We can wait for awhile but things aren't going to change," another doctor told me.

I wanted to know how long "awhile" was. Were they talking a minute, an hour, a week? I couldn't believe the matter-of-fact manner from another doctor when he pleasantly informed me, "Oh, we kept a young boy on life support for over two months once before the parents gave us permission to pull the plug. So take your time."

Next came the total melt-down, emotionally and physically. Tears were streaming down my cheeks and I blindly made my

The Only Chick in the Newsroom

way back to the ICU. I touched Ed's hand and it was warm. At one point his eyelids seemed to flutter and I felt he was trying to open them, trying to come back to me.

See, there's hope, I told myself.

I left the hospital and went home, dazed and sick. How could I possibly make the decision to end Ed's life?

There was no one to turn to, or at least, I couldn't think of anyone. My parents couldn't offer me any help. I hadn't told the children about what was happening. How could *they* understand when I didn't? I certainly wasn't going back to ask those cold, emotionless doctors for advice. So I just sat there, thinking, and praying.

I returned to the hospital the next day and happened to see one of those doctors in the hallway outside of Ed's room.

"Well, young lady, have you made a decision? Is it time to pull the plug?"

My body went limp and my legs barely functioned to get me to a bench where I collapsed and attempted to gather my thoughts. I sat there for a long time with my eyes closed, and when I opened them again I saw the doctor staring at me, and this time he touched my shoulder before he spoke.

"Make it easy on yourself. Why don't you get your hair done, or check in with friends out of town to tell them what's about to happen."

The dialogue was brutal.

Get your hair done?

Call some friends for a chat?

Was I really hearing this guy right? I knew I couldn't take one more minute of this torture.

"I can't tell you when my husband should die," I told him simply. "You make the decision and I don't need to know when." And then I went back to the ICU one final time.

Ed looked peaceful. I leaned over him, kissed his cheek, and told him goodbye. And then I left.

Ed Conway died at 4:30 p.m. that day, May 28, 1974, at the age of 48.

Thousands of people attended his Memorial Service at Trinity Cathedral in downtown Pittsburgh. Many friends stood to offer their eulogies, but the most memorable tribute came from a WTAE colleague who punctuated every paragraph, every memory of Ed, with ". . . *and there was always that smile.*"

No one who knew Ed Conway could ever forget that smile.

At the end of that long, nightmarish day, I returned home, exhausted and numb. I found myself sitting in a lawn chair on the back patio, staring at my back yard, staring at the night sky. I couldn't even cry. I just felt alone.

I don't remember much of the days that followed — just a whirl of excruciating hurt — but a week or so later, one of Ed's WTAE colleagues, Don Cannon, came by with a box of Ed's personal items. Among the notebooks and papers was a small gift box and handwritten card.

It was Ed's wedding anniversary present to me— bought, wrapped and ready, but never delivered. The gift was a ruby ring guard and Ed's World Series ring — a gift from the Pittsburgh Pirates and one of his most prized possessions. The handwritten card that went with the note was sweet and sentimental and ended with the words "the best is yet to come."

I can imagine what he would have looked like handing that gift to me, boyish and excited and eager to see my reaction. We would have laughed, kissed. I would have exclaimed over the ring, and tried it on for him. And through it all, he would have been smiling.

With Ed Conway, there was always that smile.

. . . And there was always that smile.

6
Picking Up the Pieces

*H*ow do you go on after a tragedy like that? I had lost my best friend, my life partner, and I floated to work and back each day surrounded by a hazy cloud of grief. I had survived the death of my dear baby Mary, but how many times could God expect any one person to glue her heart back together?

To make matters worse, work was no longer a safe haven. A short while after Ed's death, WIIC experienced a shake-up that would affect me personally as well as professionally. The battle for ratings was as fierce back then as it is now, and whenever ratings-trackers Arbitron or Neilson showed a station slipping a point or two, the solution was usually one of two things: Design a new set, or replace the News Director.

WIIC already had a new set. . . so the GM decided to replace By Williams. (A typically foolish decision that represents that particular GM's talent and judgment. Last time anyone heard from him he was selling cement in San Diego.)

The GM brought in a new News Director, whose name I can't bring myself to put in print. Let's just call him The Big Stupid Jerk.

Not that I want to bias you. I'm being purely descriptive.

A lot of hoopla preceded the man's arrival. It was a Monday in February when he finally came, and the weather was frigid and gloomy but we all showed up at 9 a.m. on the dot to herald the arrival. It was a lot like expecting a new baby. *What will he look like? How will he act?*

Well, we got a "baby," all right, but the kind prone to big fits and temper tantrums!

The GM introduced us all to our "new boss," and you know what they say about first impressions? Mine never wavered from the second I laid eyes on him.

You couldn't pin down his age but it was clear he was trying to appear younger than whatever he was. He had black hair that looked like it had just received a fresh coat of shoe polish, and a cheap polyester suit that was comically stretched since his hands were shoved in his pockets to avoid having to shake anyone's hand.

This man is no one's friend, he seemed to want us to understand. *This man is "all business."*

He rarely left his office, and spent most of his day at his desk clipping articles out of a stack of newspapers, sending them to the assignment desk for a crew to cover.

Boo-hoo to those high-standard news reporters who liked to waste time researching and covering their own stories! *Nosiree!* At the "new" Channel 11 news, you could figure that any story you read about in the morning paper would be the one covered on the evening TV news.

Some of us tried to pitch enterprising stories but he had no interest in anyone else's opinions. His demeanor was a fascinating display of *faux* arrogance — the kind motivated by insecurities — and anything he said to us usually was peppered with expletives, grunts, and some flying spittle.

He looked better — relatively speaking — when he was seated at his desk, when all that was visible was his shoe-polished hair and pasty skin. When he stood, he revealed the portly frame and ill-fitting clothes. Sitting or standing, though, the guy had no talent, and we all knew it. But then, he was our boss so we were bound by certain rules that go along with office protocol.

The boss may not always be right, but he always has the right to be the boss.

I was off the weekend shift, done with the wacky hours, and I liked working the Monday through Friday newscasts. If I wanted to continue to work at WIIC in peace, I pursued a path of enlightened self-interest. Which means I kept my mouth shut and my head low.

That tactic could only work for so long. I was finishing up a script one evening, on a tight deadline to have it ready for the 11 p.m., news so I didn't head out for dinner with the rest of the crew. It was quiet and I was deep in concentration, which is why I didn't hear any footsteps behind me and jumped out of my chair when I felt a tap on my shoulder.

It was him . . . the Big Stupid Jerk.

He nodded his head toward his office and I followed him there, cautious as always when dealing with him. He closed the door and stumbled through a few minutes of small talk, and all the while I kept my face blank and composed, nodding here and there but inwardly wondering what was coming next.

The answer was not pleasant.

This guy reached into a desk drawer and pulled out a tape, and casually suggested we head to an edit suite to watch it together. I looked closer and saw the tape was a well-used copy of the porn flick *Deep Throat*.

I couldn't believe it. I couldn't believe this toad of a man, this parody of a human being, had the nerve to proposition me, to suggest we sashay off to an edit suite and indulge in who-knows-what with *Deep Throat* playing in the background — just months after my husband's death, no less!

At that moment, something dark and ugly swirled around me, and an image of a long-buried memory pulled itself into shape and focus in my brain.

In this memory, I was transformed back into a twelve-year-old version of myself, and I was in the waiting room of a dentist's office in downtown Pittsburgh. Mother had decided I was old enough to go there alone, and I was feeling so proud that I didn't really think anything was amiss when the office was empty of everyone except the dentist himself, and he ushered me into the room to begin his exam.

He told me he wanted to help me relax, and he started to massage my cheek, then stroke my hair. All the while he told me to keep my mouth open and he appeared to be checking my teeth, but the caresses got more insistent and the look in his eyes scared me. He was a huge man with big hands, and I was afraid he could crush me if he wanted to.

"Aha, two cavities!" he exclaimed between silly jokes and heavy caresses. "Before I use the drill, let me help you relax some more."

He touched the fabric of my skirt, then lifted it to press one hand against my thigh. With the other hand, he began to fondle my breasts. I felt sick and frozen in the length of the chair, and I tried to ask him to stop but my voice was tiny and swallowed up by fear.

I was 12 years old!

He told me I could leave but that I'd just have to come back the following week for him to fill those cavities, and I shoved past him and ran out the door. At home, shaking and crying, I told Mother I hated the dentist, but she just explained in her gentle and loving way that many people were afraid of the dentist and that I'd have to go back.

I didn't know how to explain what had happened. I wasn't even sure what had happened; I just knew that man had his huge, frightening hands on me in ways that he shouldn't.

There were no child advocates in the 1940's, and no one spoke out about sexual abuse. Despite the tears and the pleas, Mother made me go back to that dentist two more times, and the same thing happened at each visit.

While facing that disgusting pig of a News Director, waving his cassette of *Deep Throat* in my face, I was suddenly reliving those terrifying moments in the dentist office thirty years earlier. That same feeling of being trapped engulfed me, that same feeling of being reduced and abused spread through to my bones.

Only this time, I wasn't a child. I was a woman with a voice, and I was able to fight the battle — the battle with the News Director, and the battle on behalf of a young girl still chilled by events of the past.

I shrieked at him, "Don't you dare ever insult me like this again!" then ran out of the office and slammed the door in his face.

I spent the entire night crying and figuring out what I wanted to do next. My male colleagues, dear friends and decent guys, were outraged on my behalf, but they didn't support my decision to report the incident to the General Manager.

"Ignore it," they advised. It was a case of *he-said-she-said* and we all knew the GM wasn't playing with a full deck, either. The News Director would just deny the accusation and the GM probably would fire me.

So I did swallow my anger — and a lot of my pride — and tried to put the incident behind me, but it soon became clear that the News Director was not about to forget my rejection of him so easily.

Within days, he posted a new schedule, and *surprise surprise*, I was put back on weekend duty *plus* I was given the kind of field reporting assignments usually reserved for rookie reporters. He clearly intended to make my life miserable, and he was already starting out pretty successfully at it. I decided not to stick around to see what else he had in store for me.

I quit. No regrets, no recriminations. I figured I'd rather be out of work than abused and manipulated by my boss, but as luck would have it, I wasn't out of work long. The Westinghouse revolving door swung open for me again when the General Manager of KDKA Radio approached me with an offer to be the newscaster during the morning radio drive slot — a great opportunity since it was during the highly rated Jack Bogut Show. Bogut had a folksy, down-home kind of humor, with an emphasis on storytelling that played well with the Pittsburghers listening while they sat in bumper to bumper morning traffic.

A chance to do radio seemed like the best of both worlds, to me. I loved gathering and writing news *and* being able to hide behind a microphone when I delivered it, foregoing the primping with hair and make-up that had become such a focus in television news.

The one drawback: Who could have anticipated what it would be like to have to wake up at 4 a.m. every day?! I soon discovered I could shower, dress and be in my car within fifteen minutes. I didn't hit much traffic at 4:15 so I could zoom into the city in no time and be at my desk in Gateway Center at 4:30 sharp.

On my way to the radio newsroom, I had to pass in front of the glass-fronted studio where Perry Marshall was finishing up his overnight show. Perry had a great sense of humor and I became the brunt of one of his running jokes.

"Here comes Eleanor . . . sippy cup in hand!" he told listeners, and for background music he cued up "The Stripper," and he'd include details like, "She's wearing a sweater over her blouse today to cover the coffee stains, folks!"

It was liberating to go without the usual on-air grooming but I did attempt some general sprucing up during short breaks between the newscasts, so I'd be fairly presentable by the time the rest of the staff arrived at 8 a.m.

But the breaks were short, because I had a heavy workload that included clearing the overnight wire stories, hooks for

Barbara Walters - one of the hardest working women in broadcasting. She has earned her success with an unequalled dedication to her profession.

Sam Donaldson speaking to cancer survivors

▲ Actor Karl
Malden on the
set of Lifequest

Mike ▶
Wallace -
When you talk
about gravitas.
He has it. At
age 88 he
announced his
retirement in
Spring of
2006.

▲ *Dr. C. Everett Koops U.S. Surgeon General - spending a day with him is like trying to keep up with the Energizer Bunny*

Doctor Dean Ornish ▶

▼ *Jack LaLanne - Going strong at 92*

▲ *Robin Roberts co-anchor Good Morning America*

▲Art Linkletter - a national treasure. We shared the honor of being the recipients of the first "Excellence is Ageless" award in 2005.

Shirley Jones - ▶ Our paths first crossed over fifty years ago. It was obvious to me then that she was destined for stardom

Elke Sommer on the set of Good Day Pittsburgh
Actor Jackie Coogan

▲ *Deborah Norville Inside Edition host*
▼ *Paula Zahn CNN News Anchor*

▲ *Andrew Lloyd Webber, Eleanor and Jack*

◀ *Benny Goodman - still making music in his 80's*

▲ *Eleanor surrounded by Pittsburgh's top anchor women. Left to right — Sheila Hyland, Sally Wiggin, Eleanor, Patrice King Brown, Peggy Finnegan*

▲ Lynn Swann

Marlo Thomas - ►
She will always
be "That Girl"

▲ *Receiving a Humanitarian Award from Dr. Norman Vincent Peale*

It would be unimaginable to write about my life in television without mentioning Fred Rogers . . . He was my friend from the first day I met him at the WQED studios in 1954 to the last time I saw him in the hallway at the WQED studios just before his death in 2003. Even Dr. Everett Koops was a friend of Mr. Rogers Neighborhood. ▶

▲ *Robin Leach - Champagne wishes - caviar dreams*

Does anyone remember Hedda Hopper, Hollywood's original gossip queen?

◀ *Tony Curtis*

▼ *Bob Hope*

▼ *Linda Evans - former "Dynasty" star*

▲ *Marvin Hamlisch - composer/ conductor Pittsburgh Symphony Pops*

▲ *Bill Moyers, PBS Television Journalist*

national, international, and local stories, weather, kickers. I wrote the news and delivered it starting at 5 a.m., but once KD announcer Ed Shaughnessy showed up for his show, I'd continue the writing but alternate with "Uncle Ed," as he was called, for the broadcasts.

I liked this new routine. It was different, but it was just the shift in gears I needed to help me move to a new place in my life. The hours, though, continued to be rough.

Consumerism was becoming a big feature on newscasts by the mid-'70's and KDKA TV decided they needed a consumer affairs editor so they tapped me on the shoulder just about the time when I decided I couldn't handle the 4 a.m. shift any longer. As hard as he tried, Jack Bogut never could convince me that coming to work before dawn each day was a treat.

"Eleanor, looking out over the two rivers merging into the Ohio and seeing the sun slowly peek its head over the hills is like watching each petal of a rose opening in the fresh morning dew!" he'd tell me.

I could appreciate his poetry, but it just wasn't enough to convince me. I made the jump to KD TV, and for more than a year I worked on both the TV and radio sides of the business. I anchored the morning news on the Jack Bogut show and the rest of the day I spent developing the consumer report for the TV news.

For the consumer spots, I was sent to WBZ in Boston for a quick training session with a reporter who'd been doing consumer reports for some time with great success. She was just wrapping up a week long series and was testing a pen that promised to write for a mile, and as I watched her scribble on and on for 5,280 feet, I wondered, *What am I in for*?

It was good to be back on a normal schedule but I never really embraced consumer journalism. Thankfully it didn't last long, and I was moved back to the news side, being reunited with longtime pal Ray Tannehill, and a host of new pros, including Bill Burns who had progressed quite a bit since the days when I'd worked with him on the old WDTV show *Guest To Ghost!* Bill's daughter Patti Burns was part of the news team too and it was a treat to see "Patti and Daddy" in action.

Unfortunately, it also presented a bit of a professional problem for me. I was perceived as a features reporter, and I knew that, while I might be asked to fill in on occasion, there would *never* be the chance to become a lead anchor. Those positions were taken by Bill and Patti Burns, who controlled the market. They had the highest ratings on the Noon news of any TV station in the country, a lead they maintained on the six and eleven o'clock news as well.

It was depressing to think I'd have no chance for advancement into a spot I'd once held, a spot I'd been the first woman in Pittsburgh to hold!

By this time, WPGH TV had established itself as the region's fourth TV station, and although it was a UHF station it had a good signal and had started to develop some exciting local programming. Dick Dreyfuss was an old friend from the WDTV days, where he'd been film director. Soon after he was named Director of Programming at WPGH he called to ask if I'd be interested in hosting a daily talk show called *Good Day Pittsburgh.*

It was a magazine-format show, which meant it would have taped segments rolled in with studio segments, and Dick offered me the chance to not only be on-air talent, but the *Good Day Pittsburgh* Executive Producer.

How could I refuse?

My contract at KDKA TV was up and although I must admit I struggled with the decision to leave the big K to join the new kid in town, I took the plunge.

It was a new challenge, and a chance to flex all of my skills. I had the opportunity to cover news events in depth, and attract the big newsmakers of the day for longer interviews. The show was lively and entertaining and immediately our ratings soared.

These were the mid-1970's, the years of the great Pittsburgh Steeler dynasty, and one of the features I developed was to have the key members of the team make weekly guest appearances.

Terry Bradshaw, Lynn Swann, Franco Harris, Rocky Blier . . . these guys were my good friends, men I knew from the days when I had joined Ed at all of the sporting events.

At the time, *Good Day Pittsburgh* was the only TV talk/magazine show in town, and having this kind of control over the content was a very happy assignment for me. My daughters continued to grow into lovely young women, and it left me astounded to think I was *that* age when I'd first started working in the broadcasting business! It made me realize how long I'd been working in this business, the changes I'd seen, what it was like to go from being the only woman in the newsroom to one of several — and *far* from the youngest one at that!

If you are an anchor or talk show host in a major TV market (Pittsburgh was in the top 10 back then — down in the 20's nowadays), unsolicited job offers come your way. It's the way of the business for broadcast gypsies to move around the country in search of better jobs in bigger markets. I had many offers over the years but I never seriously entertained them. I never wanted to leave Pittsburgh. I guess you could say I was homegrown with deep roots.

But I've always felt that if something was meant to be it just happened, whether you planned on it or not. And that's exactly what happened one day in 1978. I'd been working on *Good Day Pittsburgh* for a couple of years, and it was still satisfying, still fun, but the phone rang and it was a headhunter asking me, "How would you like to be the solo anchor on the evening news at the ABC affiliate in West Palm Beach, Florida?"

It's one of those movie-moments where special effects make time stand still so the main character can take time to weigh her options. My daughters had left for college the year before. Florida had always been my family's favorite vacation spot when we were growing up and now, my aging parents were spending

▲ *Good Day Pittsburgh*

▼ *Eleanor interviewing Robert Redford. Yes, girls, he's as gorgeous as you thought.*

six months out of the year there. And ever since I'd attended college in Miami for one year before transferring to Duquesne University, I'd always had an affinity for Southern Florida.

"I'd be willing to come down for an interview," I heard myself saying to the headhunter on the phone.

I'd spent more than 25 years in the television business and thought it would be a new challenge to work in the Palm Beach market — half of which is full of glitzy, glamorous wealthy snowbirds, and the other half of which suffered from pockets of poverty and racial tension. In my heart, I also knew that if I were ever planning to make a move, this would probably be my best chance. I was over forty, and most stations aren't interested in any new hire that old.

In March of 1978, the headline in the TV column of the *Pittsburgh Post-Gazette* read, "TV Veteran Eleanor Schano Leaves Pittsburgh Market and Heads South to Anchor Prime Time News."

I settled in fairly quickly at my new station, WPEC-TV. Working and living in the tony town of Palm Beach was the stuff dreams are made of, where it was not unusual to grab lunch at Taboo on Worth Avenue seated next to Senator Ted Kennedy and then grab a quick interview with Alan Greenspan later that afternoon. My daughters would fly down often to spend time with their grandparents and me, and after the tumultuous years following Ed Conway's death, I felt life coming back into balance again.

I was the South County Bureau Chief in addition to being the solo anchor on the 6 p.m. newscast, so part of my day was spent in an office at the very exclusive Boca Raton Hotel. Trust me, every single luminary you can name has, at one time or another, been a guest at the Boca Raton Hotel and Beach Club! Once, in a single day, in a single two-hour period, in fact, I saw Jimmy Carter, Art Buchwald, Benny Goodman, Alan Greenspan and Zsa Zsa Gabor all walk by my office!

There was one atypically dreary day — they have so few in South Florida — that sticks out in my memory above all others. Outside my office door, less than ten feet away, stood Robert Redford.

I had heard Redford never grants interviews, but I thought, *oh well, might as well give it a shot. What have you got to lose*? I grabbed a microphone and recording equipment and headed out to the hall. My brain ticked off some possible interview topics as I approached him and I recalled that he was in town to talk about an environmental film. I decided that instead of pursuing the same old celebrity angle, I'd try to get him to talk by broaching a subject that was his personal passion.

I walked right up to him with a smile and said, "Mr. Redford, I am very interested in your efforts to protect the environment."

He seemed pleased that a reporter would want to ask about something so close to his heart instead of press him about his latest motion picture or main squeeze, so I whipped a couple of chairs into position and said, "I'd love for us to chat for a minute," and he grinned and nodded. We were on!

It turned out we "chatted" for about 45 minutes, and even though I kept it professional, there was that alternate soundtrack running inside my brain, and I'm amused to say it was the teenage version of myself tittering and giggling over this time spent with America's premiere superhunk! I hadn't felt that way since I was fifteen years old and lying on my green chenille bedspread in my parent's house in Greentree, gazing at a bigger than life photo of Van Johnson.

I'd interviewed heads of state, princesses, world leaders, movie stars. . . but this. . . well. . . Staring into Robert Redford's dreamy blue eyes, let's just say some days it's hard to believe you're actually getting paid to do this!

***

I don't believe I'm delivering breaking news when I tell you, Florida is hot.

And when you're having hot flashes, it feels even hotter.

Despite the fact that I was happy in my work, despite the fact that I loved being near my parents and got to see my daughters frequently, there were nights when I'd wake up in a panic. My heart would race, I'd feel anxious and sad, and at first I just attributed it to being alone.

I have always been emotionally fragile, so sensitive that the slightest hurt makes me cry. And I came from a long line of anxiety-riddled women! My grandmother had a full-time job — and by "full time" I mean 24/7 — of worrying. My mom was a pro at instilling in us the clear understanding that we could get hurt doing just about anything.

So I inherited their tendency to worry, and also, when you have a lot of turmoil in your life, it's easy to accept worrying as a natural part of the process.

But this was different. I worried about *everything*, from what I'd make for dinner to the state of world politics. I wondered if I'd made a horrible mistake in moving to Florida. I loved the natural beauty of the region but the artificial world created by the rich people of Palm Beach was light-years away from what I was used to back in Pittsburgh.

Along with the anxiety, I was irritable, had insomnia, experienced hot flashes, and watched my own moods swing erratically from one side of the emotional arc to the other, all in a matter of seconds. I may not have had such a tough time of it if I'd had other women to talk to, but I wasn't part of the rich Palm Beach crowd, and since I hadn't made many friends since moving, I felt like I wasn't really part of *any* crowd.

I believe women need other women to vent to, to help validate feelings and let you know what's normal and what isn't. Now here I was, without benefit of female pals, going through

The Change of Life at exactly the point when my life was going through so many changes. *Not* a good combination!

Frankly, I didn't have the time or patience for a mid-life crisis. Between home life and work, there just wasn't room in my schedule so I decided I'd have to postpone it or skip it entirely!

That decision helped me to assess my current situation and decide how I wanted to move forward, hot flashes and all. And I realized that I was always satisfied being a "big fish in a little pond." I had no strong desire to swim with the big fish in New York, nor was I willing to sacrifice even a slice of my personal life for professional fame.

I missed my friends. I missed my roots, my hometown. Simply put, I was homesick and I wanted to return home. And "home" was Pittsburgh.

But how? I didn't have a job in Pittsburgh, so I couldn't just pick up and leave. I didn't even know where to look for a job. I was on the verge of 50, a little too "mature" to return to television except maybe as a feature reporter. I would never have given a thought to radio if I hadn't received a chance phone call from a friend.

KQV radio's Bob Dickey ranks right up there among my oldest friends in the business, going way back to the days when I worked at WDTV on the mezzanine floor of the Chamber of Commerce Building. Bob worked on the 14th floor of that building, the home of the WJAS studios.

The gathering spot for many of us who worked at the building in those days was a drug store on the first floor, where we'd meet for coffee and "shop talk." If you've been around for awhile (like I have!) you may remember names like Buzz Aston, Bill Hinds, Al Noble, Joe Negri, Nick Perry, Marty Wolfson, Slim Bryant and his Georgia Wildcats, Kay Neumann — just some of the regulars who ran into each other daily.

Except for a stint as an on-air disc jockey, my friend Bob Dickey stuck to sales, and by the time be called me in Florida, he had become General Manager at WINS 1010 AM radio in New York City.

He understood my yearnings to return home because he had just experienced the same thing. Bob and his wife Pat wanted to move their twelve (yes, twelve!) children back to Pittsburgh, and so he accepted a position in local radio.

KQV and its sister station WDVE-FM were owned and operated by Taft Broadcasting Company, who had made the decision to move KQV to an all-news format. Coming back to manage the all-news operation was a huge challenge and Bob Dickey knew it. What he didn't know was that the station was not fiscally sound and some changes in ownership were a real possibility.

I was just wrapping up the last edit on a script for the 6 o'clock news at WPEC when Bob called, telling me Taft was negotiating the sale of KQV and he was interested in taking over the ownership but he needed an "angel" to consummate the deal. We mused on who we knew who had deep enough pockets and an interest in partnering to buy a less-than-solvent radio station.

I was ticking off a list of venture capitalists, bankers, notable entrepreneurs, when all of a sudden the light bulb went off. One of the richest men in the country lived right in Pittsburgh, a man who owned and published the *Pittsburgh Tribune-Review* and another newspaper in California.

"What about Dick Scaife?"

Great idea, but how do you just call, out of the blue, Richard Mellon Scaife, a man born into the Mellon family dynasty built on American oil and banking, and ask if he's interested in partnering with you to purchase a Pittsburgh radio station?

You don't.

You look for an intermediary and after some digging, Bob Dickey found the connection in Terry Slease, a lawyer who at the time had Scaife's ear. Within months, the deal was consummated, with Richard Scaife the major stockholder and

Bob Dickey getting a minority ownership and the title of President and General Manager.

Bob and I talked frequently over the next several weeks. I needed to use this connection because I was getting more and more desperate to return to Pittsburgh, but a woman in her late-40's had little chance to getting offered anything other than a second-level position. The reality is that managers were either forced to keep women on staff for fear of an age discrimination suit, or they were looking for a spot to move them one rung down the ladder. I guess I didn't even want to face the rejection so I avoided putting out any feelers to the Pittsburgh TV stations.

I laid it on the line and told Bob flat-out I was ready to come home and I needed a job. We talked briefly about an anchor position for me at KQV and, although he never came right out and said it, I knew he wasn't quite ready to put a woman's voice on the air of an all-news station. The [misdirected] theory goes that a woman's voice just doesn't carry the authority of a man's voice.

I must assume that compassion had something to do with the next chapter of my life unfolding. Either that or I finally beat him down because on September 15, 1982, I went on the air as KQV's first full-time, prime-time female news anchor.

To set the record straight, *today* KQV has several female voices on air in addition to several senior level management positions held by women, as well as women in the sales force. Perseverance prevails, but twenty-five years ago it was a novel experiment.

For me, it was *novel* in several ways, first in fighting the attitude that a female voice can't carry authority, but also in the unusual fact of a TV broadcaster making the leap to radio. In most cases, it's the other way around; people use radio as a stepping stone to get into TV. The pace took some getting used to. Being the anchor on an all-news station barely allows enough time for a "potty break," let alone an actual coffee break — and

riding the air waves

138

heaven forbid should you attempt a full-scale lunch break! Most days lunch consisted of those awful orange cheese and peanut butter crackers!

But I was back in the city I loved! It was good to reacquaint myself with the city, and to reconnect with old friends — something sorely lacking from my life in Palm Beach. I was having lunch with one of my dearest girlfriends not long after my return to Pittsburgh when she mentioned a mutual friend who had passed away awhile back, during the time I'd been working in Florida. Verny Feeney and her husband Jack traveled in the same social circles so I'd encountered them often and, although we weren't close friends, I liked and admired the couple and was saddened to hear of Verny's death.

Jack Feeney was a prominent lawyer so his name was familiar for that reason alone, and since I had some legal matters that required advice, I decided to call Jack, not just for professional reasons but also to offer my sympathies about Verney. I expected a brief telephone conversation but Jack and I connected in that phone call. We chatted and chatted and then he suggested we meet for drinks after work.

My first impulse was to tell Jack *no*, but then a little voice in my head urged, *Go ahead, do it*, so Jack and I agreed to meet at The Top of The Triangle, a one-time famous restaurant at the top of the U.S. Steel building. I got there shortly after I finished the 6 p.m. news at KQV, and Jack was already waiting at the bar.

He looked great in his lawyer "uniform." Navy blue pin stripe suit, button-down oxford shirt and a red tie. After an eight hour shift reading the news in a tiny studio all day, trust me, I have looked better. Not expecting to stay in the city after work, I was hardly dressed for cocktails in a fancy restaurant. That morning I'd thrown on a pair of khakis, a turtleneck sweater, and my old worn-out raincoat.

We started to talk and never *stopped* talking . . . about our kids, his work, my work. The night just slipped away. We moved from the bar to a corner table for dinner, lingering over coffee until 2 a.m. I'd never experienced anything like it in my life! My daughters were ready to call the police since it was not my normal habit to be out that late without calling home.

"Where were you? How could you stay out so late? Why didn't you let us know where you were?" I was being admonished by my children much the same way I might have admonished them years earlier.

Jack and I saw each other the next night, and the night after that, and the night after that, before he had to leave for a two-week trip to the Orient. I figured I'd revel in thoughts of our recent pleasant get-togethers until he returned, so imagine my surprise when I got a phone call from Jack in Hong Kong promising to see me again as soon as he was back in Pittsburgh. *He was thinking about me too!*

You know how sometimes you can slip your foot into a shoe and know instantly that it's a good fit? Jack and I knew instantly that we were a "good fit." There was never any talk of commitment; we just assumed we'd be together as much as possible, which turned out to be just about every evening for dinner over the next months.

The Feeneys had a lovely farm in the mountains and we spent lots of weekends there during the Spring of 1983. One Sunday evening, driving home on the PA Turnpike at mile marker 82, Jack asked me to marry him. Guess that's how lawyers are: Just get the case wrapped up, doesn't matter that the PA Turnpike may not be the most romantic spot for a proposal.

I said yes.

I'd never been so sure of anything in my life. Jack was the man who could make my world complete. And I think this proved my theory that Love finds you when you aren't particularly looking for it. Somehow as I sit at my computer now, recalling our "courtship," I reflect on the past and wonder if God blessed me by saving the best for last.

July 2, 1983

Our engagement was joyous news for our families. Jack had four children, three sons and a daughter. I had my two daughters. They were all adults, ranging in age from twenty-three to thirty, and marriage brought us together in what is today referred to as a "blended family."

Funny thing was, the whole brood could have started a wedding planning business that year, because mine and Jack's engagement sparked off a case of wedding fever! Jack's daughter Erin already was planning a wedding for April. *Then* my daughter Jennifer planned her wedding for June. Jack and I chose July for our nuptials, and my other daughter Lorie decided to get married in September.

It was a crazy, joyous time, especially the day of July 2, our wedding day — just one month before my 50th birthday and one *day* before Jack's 55th birthday.

Jack's oldest son Mickey already was married, with children. The other two boys, Pat and Terry, were out of college and on their own, but in spite of the 'wedding fever' gripping our family,

▲ *Terry, Erin, Lorie, Pat, Mickey, Jennifer, Jack, Eleanor*

they decided to remain bachelors for awhile longer, moving out to San Francisco, where they would eventually meet their brides-to-be in the City by the Bay.

In a funny side-note, the "wedding fever" eventually gave way to "baby fever," as Erin, Jennifer and Lorie all gave birth to baby girls within three months of each other!

That first Christmas we spent together as a family, I decided to have both Christmas Eve and Christmas Day dinner at our house. It was a little hectic but I felt such ecstatic joy sitting around the table surrounded by a wonderful husband, children, grandchildren and my parents. Mother and Dad were in remarkably good health at the time at the age of 77 and 78 respectively.

We all learned a lot of lessons about tolerance, understanding and dedication. We are dedicated to our family as a whole and we are a whole family. As of this writing, I will proudly tell you that we have six children. It's not *his four* and *my two*. We also have sixteen grandchildren . . . all but three born on my watch.

I often think most of the credit for our success has to go to our children. There has never been one moment when any of them have ever shown one slight bit of jealousy or competitiveness. They respect each other and respect the two of us.

To mine and Jack's credit, we have worked to be completely fair and honest and open. I can't say enough about being honest and open. In a blended family, there cannot be secrets on either side, and Jack is the most principled, fair and honest person I have ever known. . . the kind of values that make for a true soul mate.

I feel our family is proof that the true definition of love is trust and respect.

Jack and I made a good team right from the start. I was the impatient, impulsive member of the team; Jack provided the calming influence that kept our relationship anchored. But he also introduced me to a world of new experiences, and, despite hectic work schedules, we indulged in new hobbies and great adventures.

Since his days in the navy Jack loved boats and yearned to own one. He finally indulged that desire but one was not enough. He became part of a yacht chartering business in the U.S. Virgin Islands, and we ended up owning four boats at one time. The cruise experience was great, however; I have always said the only way our marriage survived is because I never asked Jack exactly how much money we lost on the venture.

His next passion was bicycling. I hadn't ridden a bike since I was ten but back in the saddle I found myself at the age of 55.

"You have to wear a helmet," Jack insisted.

"I don't do helmets at my age."

It was a bit of a confrontation but he won and I wore a helmet as I rode a ten-speed mountain bike everywhere—and I do mean *everywhere*. We did one bike trek through the Napa Valley of California and two in Europe. For those of you who think you can't start a new, physically demanding hobby at this stage of your life, I can only tell you to go for it! If I could do it...you can do it.

Those early years of our marriage were filled with promise. Our children continued to provide us with grandchildren to adore, and Jack marked an enormous accomplishment in his career: He was appointed by then-Governor Dick Thornburg to the bench, as a judge in the Allegheny County criminal court of Common Pleas.

All of this started me thinking more seriously about my own career. I'd been content at KQV, I enjoyed my job anchoring the news, and even though I'd spent most of my professional life in television I found the immediacy of radio to be compelling. (Today, with modern technology, satellites, etc., TV can do it as well, but that was not true in the mid-1980's.) Reporting the news as it was happening — from my mouth to your ears — was riveting. But the hours were long — very long.

What were the alternatives? Should I hang 'em up, maybe take my skills elsewhere, say, public relations or community advocacy? I toyed with other things I could do besides broadcasting. I didn't think too much about returning to television because I wasn't even sure I *wanted* to return to television. As much as we all hate to admit it, when you're over fifty, you have embarked on the third age of life. For a woman over fifty who works in television, you might as well be in your third *billionth* age of life.

Some people asked if I considered retiring but my first response was always, "Retire *from what*? How can you retire when you feel like you've never worked a day in your life?"

And that's the truth. I am as passionate about my work now as I was over fifty years ago when I first set foot in a television studio. Oh, the job has its challenges, and its fair share of frustrations, but it has never felt like a chore.

I guess that realization gave me my answer. I wasn't ready to be done with television yet. The problem was, perhaps television was ready to be done *with me!*

I knew I was no longer considered marketable TV talent. Very perky young women were flooding the local news scene as reporters just waiting for the chance to slip into an anchor chair. I traveled around the country a lot and every time I turned on a TV the proof was right in front of me: The trend in local markets across the country was an anchor desk with *two* chairs, and one was generally occupied by a jowly, paunchy middle-aged man and the other was occupied by News Reporter Barbie. It reminded me of a CEO with his third trophy wife. (I'm relieved to say this wasn't a trend often indulged in the local Pittsburgh market!)

Up until that point in my career when one door closed another always opened but I sensed being fifty-eight meant the broadcasting door had closed on me for good. *Ahhh* how nice to know life can still be unpredictable, even when we think we know it all!

Like so many other moments in my life, it all started with an unexpected phone call on an unremarkable day. I couldn't mistake the voice at the other end of the line. It belonged to Michael Fields, who had been a producer at KDKA-TV in the days when I'd first known him, but now he was the General Manager of WQEX, the sister station to Pittsburgh's public television station WQED. The reason I couldn't mistake Michael's voice — and anyone who's ever met him can back me up on this — is because Michael is a true original. It's been said that if hummingbirds were people, they'd be Michael Fields, always buzzing around with a purpose, with a new idea, and a rapid-fire way of delivering it. In an age when General Managers were coming out of the Sales department, understanding nothing but the bottom line, Michael was still an old-school broadcaster. He loved to make TV programs, knew what it took, understood what an audience would like to see, and was willing to take risks on new ideas that might attract different audiences. Now he was asking if I could meet with him.

Over lunch, barely before the waiter arrived at our table, Michael was asking, "How would you like to discuss a new TV program I have in the pipeline? It's a live, prime-time talk show, where the audience can call in with questions for the guests."

Michael already had a name for the show. It would be called *Agewise* and here's the kicker: It would be a program targeting the *over-fifty* audience.

Pittsburgh's population was aging, and Allegheny County claimed the second-highest rate of senior adults in the country, right behind Miami, Florida. Michael's vision was a television program that provided information ranging from health and finances to social topics and occasional celebrity guests, the first program of its kind in the country with a mission to improve the lifestyle of older adults.

"And you'll be the host."

Michael Fields always dressed immaculately, right down to his crisp bow tie, and now he sat there, posture perfect, face expectant, waiting for me to answer. I thought jumping up and dancing on the tables was a little much, so I just told him yes.

A TV show for people over fifty. *That's me!* I marveled as I left that lunch and headed home. I could go back to television totally being myself. I learned a long time ago that the only way you could survive on television is if you don't try to fool the viewers, because they can spot a phony faster than they can click a remote. But on *Agewise*, I could face the viewers and act my age, laugh lines, age spots and all!

Some of my media-savvy friends cautioned me to reject the position, that tying myself to a "senior citizen" show would buy into old age.

"You don't want to give the impression you're past your prime. You can still do so many things," they told me. "Why become associated with a program on aging?"

My answer was, "Why not?"

After all, I am who I am. My mission would be to dispel those stereotypes and demonstrate the positive aspects of aging — something I felt to the depths of my soul I was capable of doing because my own life was so rich and exciting, regardless of how old I was. And I had my share of challenges, too, the kind only age and life experience can bring. I was tackling many of the topics and issues *Agewise* was being created to cover. Having adult children, building relationships with grandchildren . . . having a semi-retired husband working out of a home office . . . and the most difficult, meeting the demands of my aging parents.

Who *if not me* would be qualified to host this show?!

I was on a quest to deliver valuable information about staying healthy and growing older with class and dignity and enthusiasm, to help viewers age with attitude and gratitude! I wanted to host Agewise and I wanted it to be a hit.

Being at WQEX/WQED was a joy — proof that if you're patient and wait long enough life has a way of coming around full circle. I was there when WQED, Pittsburgh's public station, went on the air fifty years ago (I helped to collect pledges at its first fund-raising drive) and over half-a-century later, my career led me back to WQED.

Some of my favorite guests over the years on *Agewise* included Mike Wallace, Paula Zahn, Barbara Walters, Marlo Thomas, Shirley Jones, Sam Donaldson, Bill Moyers, Karl Malden, Deborah Norville, and C. Everett Koop. Other favorites included Art Linkletter, Andrew Lloyd Weber, and composer Marvin Hamlisch. And I really got a kick out of interviewing Linda Evans — admitting that I was addicted to watching *Dynasty* in the late 1980's!

I was less impressed with Tony Curtis, who crushed all my girlish memories of admiring him in the movies. My crew and I arrived at his lavish hotel suite to set up — and then wait more than an hour for him to show! When he finally did swagger in, he was sporting an ego bigger than the room we were in.

My cameraman had set up two chairs side by side for the interview, but Mr. Curtis took one look at the set-up and announced that he would not be seated for the interview, *and* that he didn't share the frame—meaning no one else was allowed to be in the picture with him. If I was going to interview him I would have to stand off-camera, facing him from a distance of 9 feet away.

At this point I had too much time invested in the interview to pack up and leave — my personal preference — so I decided to soldier on. He was deliberately obtuse during the interview, even going so far as to toss a couple of barbs at me when I asked a long question or one he didn't want to answer.

There's something to be said for consistency, though. He was rude and crude right up to the last minute. We packed up our equipment and were about to leave when Mr. Curtis grabbed my arm and gave me a squeeze and said, as if he were bestowing a royal honor, "Hey, how would you like to have your picture taken with me?"

How classy. . .

Believe me, when I introduced that field package during *Agewise*, I let viewers know exactly what the real Tony Curtis was like!

But you take the rough with the smooth in TV and Curtis was the exception, not the rule, when it came to guests. Some were celebrities, some professionals offering valuable advice, some were everyday people who made remarkable strides in community advocacy, but all of them proved there was no problem with growing older. The problems came when you started to think of yourself as "old."

I think one of my biggest thrills was hosting Jack LaLanne. Remember, my syndicated TV series *Gateway To Glamour* aired forty years earlier around the country back to back with LaLanne's program, and suddenly there he was on my set, expanding on his theories of longevity. The man is in his 90's and still works out two hours a day! He and his wife Elaine (yes, Elaine LaLanne!) operate several business ventures and both of them show up frequently on infomercials.

I've been doing the show for *sixteen seasons* and in that time it's changed its format from live call-in to pre-taped with video segments as well as studio guest; it's changed the set; and it's even changed its name — it's now known as *LifeQuest*.

And often it's changed its producer. For some on-air personalities, that's a bad thing. You get to know your producer, you get into a rhythm of working together, but for me, it's meant the chance to work with a series of remarkable women who have become my friends, and I cherish their presence in my life. Gina Catanzarite was the first — one of the most talented and skilled writers I have ever met — and an award-winning TV producer, with 5 Emmys and 13 Emmy nominations to date. But more than that, she is a marvelous human being. Gina and her husband Howard adopted two sons from Russia and she continued to juggle a career in television with family life in a way that is oh-so-familiar to me!

Next came Alicia Maloney, who started in TV as an intern, answering viewer phone calls when the *Agewise* format was still live call-in. She was a student at the University of Pittsburgh at the time, but continued to work in the TV business after graduation. I was blessed to have her as my producer for a time, but she too moved on and I'm proud to say today she is the producer of the live, nightly TV magazine program *ON Q* that airs on WQED. It's been an honor to watch her grow from a talented and willing intern to an accomplished, award-winning TV producer.

I can't say enough about Alicia's successor, Debbi Cassini, with whom I struck an instant bond. When Debbi left to take on the full-time care of her son *plus* pursue the adoption of a daughter (ultimately successful, bringing beautiful baby Isabella here from Guatemala) I was heartbroken to lose her as a colleague, but blessed to remain her friend. Following Debbi, Fate again blessed me with a wonderful producer, Renee Vid Colborn. Like the others before her, she's a real pro and a good friend.

If it sounds like I have adopted these women, it's because sometimes I feel like I have. I can see myself in them, hardworking, with a love of television and all that it is capable of doing when it functions at its best. I watched some of them move from single status to married, from marriage to motherhood, and I know that even forty years after I did it, that road's still a tough one. I have seen them confront illness and keep fighting; I have seen them face tragedy and move forward; I have seen them challenge pettiness and unfairness and still show up at work the next day determined to do their best because that's what the audience is expecting. They believe that's what the audience is *owed.*

Television is a *collaborative* art, so I'm going to ask you to do me a favor the next time you sit down to watch T.V. Stay for the credits. Sure, sometimes they roll by fast, but take the time to read each name and know that for every person you see on camera, there are dozens of wonderful people working *on* the other side to bring you the story, and bring it to you right.

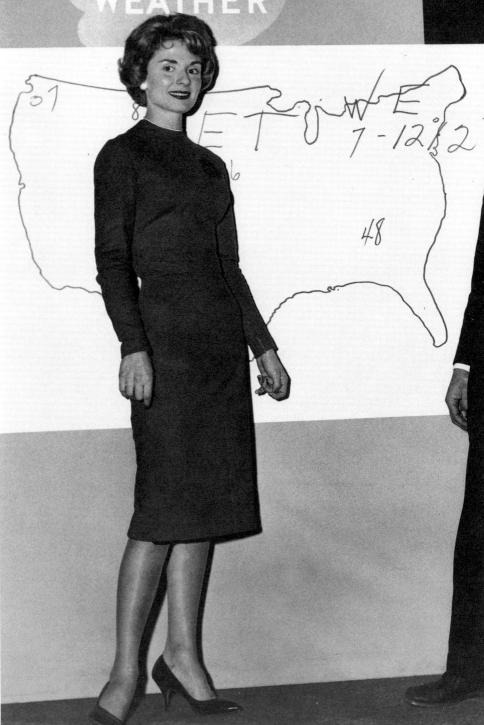

7
Into the (Gender) Gap

I've come to believe that a woman *can* have it all. She just can't have it all *at the same time*. Is that also true for men? I don't know. But I've honestly never heard a man lament the difficulties of trying to "have it all."

I'm grateful to no longer be the "only chick in the newsroom," and I am grateful to find myself working in the company of so many talented women. But we women broadcasters talk to each other, and, although our experiences vary, we often agree that there are times when it just gets a little tiring having to swim against the tide.

I think we've come a long way since the early days of overt sexism I experienced, but gender bias is still out there. Oh, maybe no one has the nerve to ask a woman to deliver the weather report wearing a negligee — but you can bet it's a common enough practice to ask a woman broadcaster to dye her hair a little lighter, tweak the wardrobe to skew a little younger.

If you don't believe me you can ask any woman broadcaster who appears on camera. If she plans on staying around for a long and satisfying career, she needs education, experience, writing skills, research savvy, good delivery — and flowing, shiny hair that sets off bright eyes and flawless skin. Long legs and high, perky breasts don't hurt, either. The demands for youthful good looks just don't seem to be the same for the men.

It's not unusual to see talented and mature women as reporters or fill-in anchors on the network news these days — but for the full-time evening anchor the scale still tilts in favor of men. When long-time Today Show host Katie Couric announced that she was leaving that position to become the first woman anchor of a network evening newscast, it was considered a watershed moment in broadcast history. The announcement was covered heavily in the media as a major news story unto itself. In this new role, will Couric be accepted and considered with the same regard accorded to such venerable network newscasters as Dan Rather, Peter Jennings, Tom Brokaw, and Ted Koppel? Or will critics ultimately say, "Katie brings a breath of fresh air to network news?" Can you imagine someone describing Dan Rather or Ted Koppel's delivery as "a breath of fresh air?"

And all the while men with receding hairlines and wrinkles deep enough to plant potatoes in are going about their business delivering the news. Hey, I don't begrudge them their ability to get on with their jobs without hassle or scrutiny. I just wish women broadcasters were free to do the same!

None of this is intended as male-bashing. It took a long time and a lot of factors to create this problem, and it will take a long time to un-do its effects. I just wish more people — *male and female* — would get on the bandwagon to put a stop to it.

Joe Rovitto, a partner at Clemenson and Rovitto, one of the leading media consulting firms in the country (and a former news director at local Pittsburgh station WTAE TV), notes that tenure and experience don't often get the respect they deserve, not just in broadcasting, but across corporate America.

"It seems Americans are obsessed with youth," Rovitto told me. "Long-term employees get 'gently pushed aside' to make room for new people with 'fresh ideas.' "

"New," i.e. *young.*

"Fresh," i.e. *young.*

In most businesses, Rovitto points out, the change in regime is a quiet company matter. Not so in television, where on-air personalities are a regular fixture in viewers' homes, so there is profound impact and high visibility when older personalities get pushed aside.

It happens to men as well as women, but perhaps it happens to women a little sooner. You'll see women anchors in their 40's and even 50's still sitting at the news desk, but it's rare to find a woman in her 60's occupying that seat. Yet you'll find plenty of men in their 60's still on air.

Rovitto sums it up nicely. "Women age. Men *mature.*"

Aging and gender in broadcast is not a new debate, nor is it a private one. It has been hotly discussed and widely argued in the public arena since the early 1980's when an anchor woman from a local Kansas TV station was fired. The reasons cited: She was "too old, too ugly, and not deferential to men."

We're talking about 1981, folks, not the Dark Ages!

The anchor's name is Christine Craft, and she carved out her own piece of broadcast history by responding with a breach of contract lawsuit against employer Metromedia. In August, 1983, amidst much media coverage, the case finally saw the light of day in a ten-day trial held at Federal District Court in Kansas City. Jurors unanimously returned a verdict in favor of Ms. Craft, awarding her $500,000 in damages — *but* United States District Court Judge Joseph E. Stevens, Jr. then threw out the verdict, and called for a second trial.

That one was held in 1984 over a six-day span in Joplin, Missouri — and again, the jury returned a verdict in favor of Ms. Craft. Metromedia appealed, and the 8th Circuit Court threw out the second verdict. The U.S. Supreme Court refused to hear the case, and so ended Christine Craft's years of litigation.

Ms. Craft still appears on air occasionally at San Francisco station KQED, and I caught up with her to ask her what she thinks about the state of media and gender bias since her landmark case.

"I see a lot more women on the air in their forties, fifties and sixties," she told me, and she says she's gratified to see the shift since there was only *one* woman broadcaster in the U.S. over the age of 39 doing a newscast in a major market (Ann Bishop, who worked at a Florida station) at the time of Ms. Craft's Federal lawsuit.

"Stations have a fear factor now, and for that I am extremely proud," she said. "But the women still have to have two facelifts to every one male facelift. So progress. . . *but* . . . you know?"

Christine Craft was a competitive surfer before she challenged what she called "that sexist nonsense and made a Federal case out of things," and when I asked her how she found the determination to press on, she simply said, "Hey, when you've seen *real* sharks, the corporate ones just don't scare you."

I've never surfed, but I like to think of that quote on days when I come up against a particularly challenging personality type!

My friends and fellow women broadcasters talk about gender bias from time to time when we get together, and when I told them about this book, and this issue in particular, many volunteered their own experiences to be included. Others voiced their experiences but said they were concerned about retribution if they went on the record with their opinions.

I'm grateful to all of them for their friendship and cooperation. Here are a few of the thoughts from women I am honored to claim as both colleagues *and* friends:

Mary Robb Jackson, General Assignment Reporter, KDKA TV

My maiden voyage in the broadcast business was as an affirmative action hire at Channel 11, then WIIC. Another woman, Linda Cooper, and I were brought in as the first two women to work on the Studio crew. I recollect walking into the studio, and seeing out of the corner of my eye, one of the crew restraining another of his union brothers who was not pleased that we had arrived. These were the kinds of jobs where, until then, when there was an opening only fathers, sons, brothers, nephews, any male etc. were considered. We had the wrong plumbing.

I'm happy to say that after their initial shock these guys were more than willing to teach us the ropes. We pulled cable with the best of them, but there were times when sexual innuendo would have to be tempered after a difficult to define line was crossed . . . but I have good memories of those times.

Linda Cooper went on to become a photographer\editor in television news, and after a stint in programming I joined her as a reporter. One morning we were assigned to interview former President Gerald Ford at the Duquesne Club. This was in the mid-70's and the club was still very much a male bastion. We walked up the front steps and were quickly turned around and told that we would have to enter using the freight elevator.

Feeling a little like second class citizens we called back to base. The assignment editor said we could make our own decision about whether to proceed. We figured what the heck. Neither of us has ever seen the interior of the Duquesne Club, what difference did it really make how we got in there. We rose to the appropriate floor in the freight elevator accompanied by a 'minder' - just in case we made a break for the smoking room, I guess. Following our interview with Mr. Ford we again descended with our 'minder.'

Now, understand that Linda is a statuesque African-American woman. At that time video equipment was heavy and quite unwieldy. It included the camera on her shoulder, a power pack on her back, a battery belt, a recorder on the other shoulder, and the tripod. I have no idea how much it all weighed. As we stood in that crowded elevator the 'minder' looked up at her (he was on the short side) and said, "What's a nice girl like you doing in a job like that?" Linda took a beat, then slowly leveled her gaze at the man and replied, "Sure beats pickin' cotton." The door opened and we exited.

These were the little victories.

As a general assignment news reporter there were times when I would be called to a press conference at Allegheny County police and the superintendent would greet me with a hug and a kiss. He was a nice man from a different generation and I initially didn't want to hurt his feelings but I could sense that my male counterparts took note. It finally made me so uncomfortable that I told the superintendent that he could continue his affectionate greetings, but only if Andy Gastrmeyer got the same. He got the idea.

I also got the sense that police especially didn't feel that crimes scenes were places for women. It was unspoken but I sometimes felt at a disadvantage. Much of that has changed and I now feel that there is far more equality in that area.

Most of what I learned as a broadcast journalist, I learned from men on the job. There have been photographers, editors, producers, and fellow reporters who have taught me a great deal - beginning with how to hold a microphone with conviction. I am forever grateful for their fine tutelage and generosity, but the mixture of aggressiveness, passion and compassion with which I do my job and the ability to tell a story well are all mine . . . I only wish that I might have received equal pay for equal work over these 31-years.

Lynn Cullen, a fixture on Pittsburgh television and radio since 1981, who currently hosts a daily three-hour radio show on 1360 WPTT.

I never would have gotten my first job in television if it hadn't been for affirmative action. I was the first on-air woman hired at WISC-TV in Madison, Wisconsin who wasn't there to do a homemaking-type show for the noon hour. The only reason I was hired was that the Federal government was holding a gun to the heads of all TV station managers to start hiring women and Blacks.

My first day on the job (this was 1975) I was greeted by a used condom in the top drawer of my desk. I'm assuming that was not the way a male hire would have been greeted. I became the first female anchor in Madison, but was summarily relieved of my anchoring duties when a new general manager took over. He felt that women didn't have "the authority or the voice" to deliver news. I immediately sued, claiming blatant sex discrimination, and was reinstated to my anchor position in a matter of weeks after a great deal of press attention and without the case ever going to court.

I don't think there's any doubt that the playing field was not level during my television career. I always felt like an exception to the rule. I still am, as one of only two full-time female talk radio hosts in the Pittsburgh market. Talk radio remains an overwhelmingly male bastion, as does radio in general. I think it's still believed that a woman voicing strong opinions is off-putting to many in the audience and I don't know that that assumption is incorrect. Men in radio who come on strong are considered tough or funny or macho. Women who come on strong are considered shrews.

A TV anecdote that occurs to me here: When [WTAE meteorologist] Joe DeNardo and I were co-hosting the Cerebral Palsy telethon, the producer asked me the day before the broadcast what shoes I'd be wearing. It seemed like an odd question to me, but it became apparent why she was asking.

"You're taller than Joe," she said, "and the two-shots don't look good."

Of course, that was nonsense. What she meant to say was, "You're taller than Joe, and women aren't supposed to be taller than men, so you'd better wear flats and slouch a lot."

If Joe had been two or three inches taller than me, she wouldn't have had any trouble with the two-shots. The problem was a woman appearing to be bigger (more authoritative, stronger?) than the man, and that was apparently not allowed. By the way, I wore two-inch heels.

I remember when I was hired at WTAE-TV in 1981, I was stunned to discover there were no women on set. It was all male. All white. All the time. I don't think that changed until about 1985 and even now, the ratio of men to women on set is usually three to one at that station. One female co-anchor, a male co-anchor, male meterologist and male sportscaster. I think the business still sees men as more authoritative than women. Look at the Sunday morning news shows. All male anchors. Look at the evening news programs—with the exception of ABC.

Obviously, there's been a lot of progress in the thirty-plus years I've been in broadcasting. It's been gratifying to see it and it's been fascinating to be on the cutting edge of it. I feel I've been very lucky.

Sheila Hyland, Pittsburgh news anchor from 1988 - 2006

I can honestly say I don't think my gender in any way prevented me from getting hired for any job, although it's usually spelled out in advance whether the station is looking for a male or female anchor. And I would say that being a female in broadcasting has made it more difficult for me in just one way: Appearance. No question. I will give you a few instances.

It started with my first job at NTV in Kearney, Nebraska (in 1984). I was hired to report, produce and anchor. But at one point our meteorologist took a vacation. My News Director asked me, with absolutely no knowledge or experience in forecasting the weather, to do the job temporarily for "cosmetic purposes." That's an exact quote.

In other words, I was young, blonde and apparently attractive enough to fill the bill! Being young and grateful to have a job, I did as I was asked. After a week of making a fool of myself in front of the weather map, I marched back into the News Director's office and told him if he ever asked me to fill in on the weather again, I would quit! He never asked me again and, in fact, promoted me a couple of months later.

My second job was at KWTV in Oklahoma City. I found out just how important appearance was when I was asked to bring in my entire wardrobe for the perusal of the General Manager and his wife! I spent an 8-hour shift doing nothing but changing outfits and accessories so that they could tell me what I was and was not allowed to wear on the air (and they didn't provide me a clothing allowance). I guarantee you the male anchors were never subjected to such scrutiny.

About a year after that, still at KWTV (around 1986), the news director called me into her office. She proceeded to ask me if I had gained weight, which I had (probably about 10 pounds). Then she told me that I needed to lose some weight. Keep in mind, I was a size 10 and no more than 20 pounds overweight total. My co-anchor was probably at least 30 pounds overweight, but his size was never questioned.

Anyway, I asked her what would happen if I didn't lose the weight and she told me I'd lose my job!! Needless to say, I dropped 20 pounds and remained a size 6 for all but the last two years of my television career. It was a humiliating and eye-opening experience.

During my tenure in Pittsburgh, I was occasionally asked to change my hairstyle. Once even asked to drastically change my hair color so that I wouldn't 'match' the color of my male co-anchor. And every once in awhile a News Director would ask me not to wear a certain outfit or accessory (once I was told not to wear dangle earrings, which I agree with—too distracting!). But I should point out again that I don't recall a male colleague being lectured about his clothing, accessories or body size. Facial hair was about the only thing that sometimes was an issue with my male co-anchors.

I didn't encounter much in the way of sexual harassment with the exception of one male co-worker who repeatedly talked about the way I looked, eyeing me up and down and making very sexual comments. I ignored it or laughed it off at first, but when I'd finally had enough, I called him on the carpet about it. He stopped the behavior and things were fine after that.

Lori Savitch, 20-yr broadcast veteran who has worked as a news reporter and anchor in Pittsburgh, Philadelphia, and Charleston, SC.

As I look back over the years in local news, the one thing that's come to mind is how the industry has changed intellectually. I started at KYW-Newsradio in Philadelphia in 1984. At that time, there were still quite a few members of the "old boys network" left, the smoking, cursing, drinking guys who remembered all too well the years when there were no women in the newsroom. I called them "grey heads" in retaliation for their name for pretty newswomen: "spray heads" — as in "hair spray."

Those old grey heads were mean, crotchety bastards. I was never sexually harassed, but they never missed a chance to tell me how stupid I was. And I guess I was stupid — but couldn't they see how hard I was trying?? I was young. I cried a lot.

But now, I see that those old grey heads were keeping to an intellectual standard that they didn't want to see slip away. They held me to that standard as well. But now that the grey heads are gone, the standard is gone, too.

On the rare occasions when I watch local news, I cringe at the poor writing. And that's because the people in charge are young. They're not stupid, they're not uneducated, they're just YOUNG. And they're running the show.

When I left local news at age 40, I was the "grande dame" of the newsroom. And, I'm afraid to say that I was sometimes as mean and crotchety as those old bastards. The intellectual bar had been lowered over the years, and it pissed me off!

I miss those mean old grey heads. They kept us youngsters in the newsroom to a standard set by the likes of Edward R. Murrow. They remembered what it was like when the industry was new. I always thought they were mean to me because I was a woman. Turns out, they were probably just pissed off that I was young.

Bev Smith, Nationally Syndicated Host of The Bev Smith Show

I first started in the Communications Business in the 1970's. It was the heart of the Black Civil Rights and the Women's Human Rights Movement. It was also a time when Ralph Nader was in the public eye revving up the Consumer Rights Movement. I was involved in every demonstration as an activist.

It was right at that time that I was named a staff reporter for the NBC Pittsburgh Affiliate, WIIC, which is now WPXI. It made all the papers. Blacks in local Media across the board were only slightly represented. My visibility became the symbol of the New Black and Women's Movement.

On the surface it looked like we were advancing as a gender and ethnic group, but the truth is it was only window dressing. Management called the shots, and our paychecks still didn't match our Male counterparts. We still had to fight for the stronger stories.

Ultimately, when the network hired a consultant to review programming, we women on the air still faced a consultant who let us know — and told everyone who listened — that he didn't want a "Black Bitch" working in his newsroom. He said this directly to my face.

It is some 25 or 30 years later and as I watch how we are portrayed I would say today things aren't much better. We are still used in token votes and with rare exception (Katie Couric and Oprah) we still aren't equal in competition.

***

I truly appreciate the opinions of my friends and colleagues. Is giving them a chance to be heard a slight detour from the story of my life? In a roundabout way, not really. Gender bias is so intricately woven into the fabric of my career that I honestly don't think I could tell my life story *without* including this chapter on the subject.

riding the air waves

Those of us who have ridden the waves together have found it therapeutic over the years to share our war stories. I know my circle of women friends has been my touchstone and barometer throughout my career, and at the worst of times, I could count on a lunch or a dinner filled with commiserating and dark humor, which made it easier to laugh off the tough times behind me and square my shoulders to meet the ones on the horizon.

So yes, hearing from them and voicing my own opinions *is* a part of my history. Am I suggesting that the experience was the same for every woman who ever worked in broadcasting? No. Maybe there are some women news reporters who sailed through their careers without encountering any gender bias at all, and to them I can only say I'm glad some women were fortunate enough to shatter the glass ceiling without getting cut in the process.

I also know other women worked in the same television stations where I worked over the years and they managed to avoid the problem of gender bias — *except* it seems to me they usually worked on the *programming* side of things, *not* in the newsroom. As television broadened its offerings over the years, the Programming department produced things like talk shows and homemaker programs, cooking and lifestyle shows. They usually aired in the daytime, so the target audience was women. You can bet no man was beating down the door to host a local homemaker show aimed at housewives.

The newsroom was different, a male bastion that wasn't quick to warm up to women competing with them for news reporter and anchor jobs.

Being one of the older women you're likely to find on the air *anywhere* in this country — and being here for the past 50+ years — I have to say the debate about gender bias always finds me an eager and vocal participant. Frankly, I *like* to see a little maturity in the men and women delivering the news. It gives me a certain comfort to know they might actually remember a war that wasn't fought in Iraq.

But it's about revenue, in the end, and television is a bottom-line business. I understand that we all like to "buy" a pretty product, and I am just as likely as the next person to skip over the dented can of soup on the supermarket shelf.

My gripe is that older women seem to automatically become the dented can of soup in this scenario! Why are women in television so frequently considered "damaged goods" just because we committed the unpardonable sin of aging?!

No matter where you live in this country, take a good look at the younger women you see on air, and yes, the smooth skin and the highlighted hair and the artful make-up create an attractive package. But also look at the older women. Tell me you aren't in total awe of CNN's Christiane Amanpour! Listen to her interview a world leader or deliver a special report and tell me for one second anyone can scrape together an argument that says viewers would rather hear news from a younger woman just because she fits neatly into pop culture's definition of beauty.

And even if "beauty" *is* the standard by which any are judging, I'd *still* put Christiane Amanpour head and gorgeous shoulders above the rest! There's a magnificent kind of beauty etched in every line of her face, in hair that may be flyaway because she's reporting from a battlefield, in clothes that may be rumpled because she's stepped from an SUV that's just crossed the border into a war-torn nation. She shines with the kind of remarkable beauty that can only come from confidence and accomplishment, and I urge you to make a conscious choice to honor that kind of talent and beauty when you're watching your daily news.

My career oftentimes has felt like I was fighting on the front lines of the war for equality, which is why I've taken the time here to share my viewpoint on this subject. Should I get back to telling you about these most recent years of my career and life? Okay. Will I ever stop speaking out for what's fair and right, in my life, or in the lives of other women battling for parity? No.

Because the bias is still out there. In some places it's subtle and in others it's as obvious as a big purple elephant in the living room. Most women are willing to bet on it. But remember to factor in the wage gap when you're placing your bets.

Currently, women still earn just 79 cents to the male dollar.

8
Re-Inventing the Art
of Re-Inventing

People like celebrity stories and they always ask me about the "famous" people I've met. I could tell them about Grace Kelly or Frank Sinatra, Robert Redford or Bob Hope. But often, as I reflect on the countless number of people I have interviewed over the years, it's the "ordinary" ones who made the most lasting impressions.

The one who drifts in and out of my memory the most is a woman I was sent to interview in the mid-1960's. Her name was Vera Murphy, and she was about to celebrate her 100th birthday. Today, that would hardly be a newsworthy event since more and more people are living to reach 100 and beyond, but back then it made a great "kicker," which is what they call a good human-interest feature that can air at the end of the evening newscast.

My cameraman and I traveled to a small rural community about 30 miles from Pittsburgh. The address we were given was hard to locate since most of the secondary roads were poorly marked and it took about an hour before we located the tiny clapboard farm house almost secluded among tall maple trees. Our travel time made us late for the appointment so we weren't too surprised when no one answered the door. We knocked and knocked until Les, the cameraman, joked, "Gee, she's 100 years old. Maybe we didn't make it in time."

Just as we were about to drive away, a tiny lady appeared from the back of the house . . . pushing a wheelbarrow full of topsoil! Vera Murphy had gray hair and a smile a yard wide and she greeted us with the explanation that she hadn't heard us knocking because she'd been out back working in her garden.

Vera shook the dirt off her apron and invited us in for a cup of tea. The small living room was tidy and the kitchen table immaculate as we began our interview. The camera rolled as she told about losing her husband, about raising three daughters, all of whom went to college, got married and moved away.

"Are you ever lonely or worried living alone in the woods?" I asked.

Vera smiled. "Why should I be lonely, I have the birds that sing, the leaves that rustle in the breeze and the sounds of nature to keep me company." For good measure, she pointed to a big German Sheppard asleep on the back porch. "And Sparky keeps me safe and secure."

I'll never forget the answer she gave to my final question. "How does it feel to be 100 years old?"

With a twinkle in her eye and a bit of a southern drawl Vera reached out, patted my hand, and replied, "Honey . . . it feels real good. . ." cause there ain't no peer pressure anymore."

Up until 1994, Mother and Dad were still living in the family home and managing pretty well in spite of Dad's declining health. If you've cared for aging parents, you know the drill: Bring a few groceries, clean up here and there. (Get chastised as if you were still a child because you aren't doing it exactly the way your parents want you to!) You watch a little *Wheel of Fortune* and you make sure they're taking their medications, and you wander around your childhood house wondering how time has flown by.

Over in that corner, the place where we took a photo of Mom, Dad, Grandma and Grandpap with me on the day of my First Communion . . . around back that hillside of forsythia where I once found a baby rabbit nestled among the leaves . . . the side porch where I spent most of the hot, sultry summer of 1942 with my swollen, itchy legs propped up on pillows after climbing a tree covered with poison ivy.

I would try to visit my parents every other day and often found myself with tears in my eyes. Everything important that had ever happened in my early life had happened in that house. Sometimes, I would sit in my old bedroom and remember all the moments of lying on the floor staring at the ceiling, dreaming of the future, or simply reading Nancy Drew books and leafing through magazines. I recalled the long hours in the basement trying to make a skirt for home-economics class. There were so many mundane things lost along the path from childhood to adulthood. Mother was an impeccable housekeeper who felt it necessary to clean out every cupboard and drawer at least once a month. The memories flooded me, whether I was consciously calling for them or not, and every time I visited I became a little closer to my childhood and a little more fearful of what the future held.

The day Dad made his last trip to the hospital in spring of 1994, none of us were prepared for what would come. He sat in his big blue recliner wearing his Irish cable knit sweater when I kissed him goodbye. I went to the WQED studios to tape my show while my sister and Mom drove Dad to the hospital. He was treated for a bladder infection, but the doctor decided to admit him for further tests, and within a few days it was apparent his condition was far more serious than we'd realized, and that he was not going to get better.

Mother, Clare and I took shifts being with him. On May 4, 1994, after they left to go home for dinner, I was at my father's bedside when he took his last breath. His passing left a gaping hole in my heart I loved my Dad and continued to dance for him until the end.

Mother and Dad had been married 66 years and as would be expected her health slowly declined following his passing. She closed up the family home in Greentree and moved to Florida to be near my brother Bob. The months turned into years and, assuming that she would not be returning to Pittsburgh, we made that heart wrenching decision to sell the family home.

My sister Clare and I spent weeks sorting through the precious mementos of my parents' marriage. The carefully preserved linens that mother was always saving "for good." Her recipes, her poetry, her collection of tea cups and miniature pitchers, stacks of handmade aprons sewn from outgrown dresses. Our adult children wanted few of their grandparents' belongings — it seemed their lifestyles just didn't include the need for fine china and crystal — so the things that had mattered so much to my parents were now about to be disposed of or donated to charity.

On that final day of closing up my childhood home, I found myself floundering through time, assailed by the crashing of past and present events, emotionally devastated and about as far from the composed and made-up on-air TV personality as you can get.

At the very end, I sunk to the floor of the basement, face, hands and jeans covered in grime, clutching the detached porcelain head of my favorite childhood baby doll, retrieved from behind a radiator, and wondered how I could walk out that door for good.

I was blessed to have Mom still alive, but I knew I would never again smell one of her dinners cooking in the kitchen, would never hear the creaking of the floorboards or the chime of the clock on the mantelpiece. When the tears started to flow, they came in great waves, pouring down my cheeks and dripping onto my hands and the long-lost baby doll's dusty head.

I cried that way for a long time, until finally I heard a sound, looked up and realized I was not alone. One of the Floor Directors from WQED, Jimmy Seech, has a hobby of restoring and selling antiques and days earlier I had invited him to stop by and see if there was anything he was interested in. He showed up at just that moment.

This kind, friendly acquaintance, who'd never seen me in anything less than full make-up and polished on-air wardrobe, came toward me holding the body of the baby doll whose porcelain head I clutched in my hands. He put a hand on my shoulder, helped me to my feet, and helped me walk out of the house. We never exchanged words about it at the time, and neither of us has ever mentioned that day since, but I think it's just another sign of a benevolent God, who sends you angels and courage and friendly Floor Directors at precisely the time when you need it most.

My childhood home was sold in a matter of days after it went on the market and to this day, I have yet to find the courage to see it again.

If the house was gone, at least I still had my mother with me. She eventually returned from Florida to a lovely apartment in an assisted living facility in Greentree. It was in the same neighborhood where we had all grown up — close to most members of the family, so she always had visits from someone she loved. We celebrated holidays and her birthdays, and for her 95th birthday we had a huge party with the whole family gathered together. My sister handled a lot of the details for that party, informing me that it would be *my* task to handle Mom's 100th birthday party.

I often thought of that Centurion I had interviewed, Vera Murphy, as I watched my mom age, convinced she too could reach 100 and beyond. Mom didn't have the spunk to push a wheelbarrow but she had the same kind of smile as Vera, wide and wonderful, and it was outmatched in brightness only by the light in her blue eyes. My mother had a gentleness and goodness and humor about her that made her the love of so many people's lives.

It's unusual to be in your 70's and *still* be someone's daughter. Not too many of my contemporaries could claim the same experience. At my own 70th birthday party, mom was right there beside me and someone asked us to pose for a picture. Afterwards I hugged her and whispered, "I can't imagine ever living without my very best friend."

I feel I received one of God's dearest gifts in allowing me to live so much of my life with my mother. Eleanor Martha Schano died on January 31, 2004, at the age of 97.

That period of time, from 1994 to 2004, has come to define my existence. It is a decade with brackets at each end that left me an orphan. It is a decade that left me thinking about time, about all that it affords us, and all that it does to crush us.

In television, time is absolute. Programs, commercials, promotions are scheduled right down to the nano-second, so throughout my career I lived with a stopwatch as my best friend.

That has a way of spilling over into your personal life, so you can bet I spent the past decades as an obsessive clock-watcher even when I wasn't at work. Recently, when my schedule got particularly hectic, my memories drifted back to a best friend from years ago, and how she reacted when she was diagnosed with breast cancer. She threw her watch away and turned all the clocks in her home to face the wall.

It was a bold move, living the spirit of a quote by the Greek philosopher Seneca, who said, "When shall we live if not *now*?"

Ah ha. . .

What would it be like to spend one entire day without wearing a watch, without constantly gazing at a clock or the Palm Pilot or DayTimer or Blackberry and wondering what we were late for, where we had to be next?

I decided to give it a try. Instead of a jarring alarm clock, I let the sunshine streaming through the window wake me up. I lounged on the bed, read the Sunday paper, had brunch with my husband Jack, and lingered over a second cup of coffee.

Next came a walk — no pedometer clipped to my belt, just a stroll through the neighborhood. If I wasn't counting the seconds, why bother counting my *steps*, right? I could hear the birds chirping, the breeze blowing, but at times even those were still, and the only thing playing through my mind was the gentle chant, "*Now.*"

Reality came crashing back the next day, of course . . . phones ringing, appointments calling, work demanding, and the clocks all around me tick-tick-ticking. But what a wonderful experiment, inspiring me to find more times in my life when I would permit myself to stop watching the clock and just *live*.

I wonder what would happen if we also took a break from *watching the calendar*, too.

I'm asked to do many speaking engagements these days and when it comes to the topic of aging, I ask my audience, "If you didn't know how old you were, how old would you feel?"

That question always produces some jaw-dropping. *I never thought of it that way.*

If I had to pin it down, I'd say I feel about 20 years old — the same as when I stepped into that TV studio for my very first audition. (Oh, I don't feel so naïve, and believe me, *that's* refreshing. Youth isn't always what it's cracked up to be!) But cover up the calendar and ask me how old I *feel*, and I'll tell you straight out that I feel no real difference now than I did then, in how I want to meet the world, how I want to roll up my sleeves and get to work every day, how I hope that love, beauty, friendship and family continue to bless my life.

I don't really discuss my age, to tell you the truth, and over the years, some folks made the natural assumption that it was because I was trying to hide it. Not true. I just never really felt it had much impact in defining who I am, and I hate the way someone hears a certain number and immediately attaches some misguided perception of "old age" to it.

Funny how our attitude about aging changes dramatically as we grow older. At least mine has. I remember when I thought forty was really old! I never thought I'd be loving the age that I am in my 70's but it's the best place I've ever been.

When I speak to groups, people often ask for my advice on aging with such energy and *gratitude*, and the only advice I can give is that gratitude is what got me here in the first place. Every morning, before I get out of bed, I thank God for the blessings and opportunities He will give me this day. My wonderful friend Bonnie Hasson — the best Reiki practitioner around — taught me that prayer. Instead of thanking God *after* He has given you a blessing, try thanking Him upfront.

And yes, *Reiki*. It's one of the more widely known forms of energy healing, and I practice it regularly, along with yoga, Pilates, and cranio-sacral massage, another Naturopathic therapy. And in case you think you're too old to take up any one of those disciplines, let me tell you that the best yoga teacher I ever had is now 86 years old, and my goal is to be able to do even half as much as she can do!

My personal philosophy is simple. God gave me a healthy, strong body, and it's my responsibility to take care of it. It whispers *Good job, Eleanor!* after a three-mile walk and *What the heck were you thinking?!?!* after I give in to a Twinkie craving.

Personally, I hate to hear people complaining all the time about the things their bodies can't do anymore. I suggest celebrating the things it can do instead. I recall one night returning home after a hectic ten-hour day and announcing to my husband Jack as I walked in the door, "I just love my body." That declaration left Jack more than a little surprised so I explained the *Why* behind it.

I had driven over a 100 miles that day to deliver a keynote speech and had raced home again to emcee a fundraiser that same evening. My body had performed beautifully all day long, allowing me to drive my car, race up six flights of stairs when I was running late, provided me with the stamina to lift and stretch and walk and talk. Maybe we should all pause occasionally to give our bodies a mental hug.

I think one of the best things about growing older is you care more about how you *feel* than how you *look*. There is no substitute for just staying healthy, so good whole foods, exercise and a huge helping of enthusiasm make up for any lines and wrinkles.

I can recall strolling on the Carnegie-Mellon University campus in the summer of 2005, when the National Senior Olympic games were being held in Pittsburgh. I stopped by the stadium to watch men and women in excellent shape throwing discus, warming up for softball. And then over the P.A. system I heard the announcement, "In the 90 to 95 year old age group . . . will the women competing in the 100 meter dash please report to the starting gate."

There they were, six of them, lining up, flexing their muscles, all decked out in their running shoes and some nifty silver streaks in their hair. And you know what? They did just fine. If you want to be the one to tell them they're old, give it a shot — *if* you can catch up with them!

As I come to the close of this memoir, I want to leave you with the challenge to always think about how old you *feel*, not how old you *are*. When I was just starting my career, my actual age may have been *young*, but I relied on *feeling older* to pull me through, even if I didn't have the experience and wisdom that comes with age. Now that I'm *older*, I rely on the courage, drive and big dreams that usually motivate a person when she's *young*.

It's one of life's funny little ironies, I suppose, but hey, it's gotten me this far, and I hope it takes me much farther!

From the beginning — over fifty years ago — I never believed anyone when they told me I couldn't do something. I'd just find a way, or accept that Fate would find a path for me, and I never, ever *lost* my enthusiasm for what it was I set out to do. I do it a little *differently* now. I no longer put in 12-hour days, I no longer skid into my house at the end of the work day only to switch hats from "on-air talent" to "mommy." But I don't regret that I did it that way. My daughters — the same girls I carted to work with me so many times when they were young— recently told me they don't have much memory of me having a job. *Can you believe it?!* I can only say that must be proof that whatever I did worked out just fine for my family. I struggled and juggled so I could be there for them at the most important times and that's what they remember. — my being there for them. For that I am grateful.

I am equally grateful that my friends and fellow television viewers of Pittsburgh remember me being there! As broadcast journalists, we are in so many people's homes that we sometimes become a *de facto* part of the family. I have always considered it flattering to have people call out to me in a crowded store or on a street corner, "Hi, Eleanor!"

I can only take it with a grain of salt when, every once in awhile, a viewer asks a question that defies a quick answer. My favorite is, "Didn't you used to be Eleanor Schano?"

Used to be, still am, I want to say, but I just smile and nod.

Once while waiting for my luggage at an airport baggage claim I felt a young man staring at me and when he finally approached me he asked, "Didn't you used to be somebody?"

I smiled and extended my hand and said, "Hello. My name is Eleanor Schano," to which he gave me one last look and said, "No, that's not it," and picked up his suitcase and walked away.

How can you feel slighted by something like that when it's just so darn funny?!

I guess there's a lot of responsibility that comes with a job that puts you in the public eye. But we *are* real people, who laugh and cry our way through life, just like everyone else. We sit at the bedside of a loved one in the hospital, we hold the hand of a dying parent. We go to the grocery store in sweatshirts and jeans and when someone asks, "Hey, aren't you Eleanor Schano?" you feel like saying, "No way." We mess up recipes when we cook, we worry about our kids, we spoil our grandkids, we're devastated if a pet has to be put down. I hope what you've read in these pages helps you to realize that the reporters reporting the human interest just happen to be human themselves.

Oh, you find those rare ones who are there to exploit, out to hurt. Fred Friendly was the former president of CBS News in the 1950s, and later was news producer at NBC. Friendly once said, "Because television can make so much money doing its worst, it spends little time doing its best."

One of the reasons that I wrote this book is because I wanted viewers to know that every day that I work in broadcasting, I am doing my best to bring accurate and interesting stories to the public. Too often, people give it their all for their pet projects, their personal favorites, and then just "phone it in" for the other stories. But I try to treat each story the same, research and write it and tell it well, whether it's about a U.S. President or a Vera Murphy.

I also wrote this book for my daughters, my granddaughters, my girlfriends, and all the women who are following behind me — traveling a path that I hope will be somewhat smoother than my own.

But if it's *not* smooth, I'll tell you to follow it anyhow! Find something you are truly passionate about, get the best education you can, and then just *do it*. Do what you love, no matter who tells you that you can't, no matter what reasons they give you, and if you do I assure you that, like myself, you'll never feel like you "worked" a day in your life.

Do you recall the anecdote I told at the beginning of this book, the one about the woman in the grocery store who asked my friend if she knew "the real Eleanor Schano?" She was convinced that Eleanor Schano, like Betty Crocker, was just a character that many women had played over time. I wish I could find that woman now. The more I think about it, the more convinced I am she was right.

There *have* been a lot of Eleanor Schanos: The little one who thought she was Brenda Starr. . . the model shaking as she auditioned for her first TV speaking role. . . the starry-eyed bride . . . the weather girl in a negligee . . . the mother sobbing when her daughter died. . . the grieving widow . . . the broadcast pioneer. . . the PTA mom. There have been Eleanor Schanos at the most elegant fundraisers and Eleanor Schanos leading the Girl Scout troop. The Eleanor who was unsure, and the Eleanor determined to take on the world.

In more than half a century lived in the public eye, you get to be a lot of different versions of yourself. And hopefully each new version is a little bit wiser than the one that went before.

Thank you for reliving this journey with me, for meeting *all* of the Eleanors who have lived in these pages. I hope at moments my own experiences offered you inspiration, at some points a glimpse back at broadcast history, a few fond memories, and at the very least a couple of good laughs here and there. I hope you are inspired on some level to tell your own stories, to continue to evolve into wiser, more mature — but never old —versions of yourself!

Writing and re-reading my own life story has been hard, but worth it. I *like* the Eleanor Schano I am now. And I look forward to meeting all of the Eleanor Schanos yet to come. Today happens to be one of those days when I am not checking the clock, not looking at the calendar. The future is spread out before me and I still have big plans. And great faith.

So thank you. And stay tuned.